10/25

£ 10.00

02/101

CW01637501

TRANSITIONS

EACH TRANSITION CAN BE AN UPDATE
TOWARD YOUR BEST VERSION

Dear Peter

Thanks for all what you are doing to bring more awareness on narratives silenced in the Middle East!

Keep it up!

Hamza

:)

TRANSITIONS

EACH TRANSITION CAN BE AN UPDATE TOWARD YOUR BEST VERSION

AUTHORED BY

HAMZA GHANDOUR

penmanbooks.com

Penman Books

Office No. 303, Kumar House Building,
D Block, Central Market, Opp PVR Cinema,
Prashant Vihar, Delhi 110085, India
Website: www.penmanbooks.com
Email: publish@penmanbooks.com

First Published by Penman Books 2020

Title: Transitions
ISBN: 978-93-90156-56-6

Contents

Thankful

Being thankful is not only about great memories but also about being grateful for each moment and experience and how they shape you into becoming a better person. On a personal level, I am thankful for having a supportive family, close friends and for discovering myself and experiencing life within lofC at a whole different level. I am thankful to everyone who has supported me and has been there for me through it all. Each relationship has added a new flavor to my life and knowing that many people are going to stay with me through it all, makes me eternally grateful. Thankful as well to all those people who entered my life to teach me a specific lesson at a certain period of my life.

لبنان المحبة

الرحلة بلّشت بشارع المحبة
شارع مشعشع
لا بيعرف تفرقة دينية ولا تفرقة سياسية
شارع مليء بالإنسانية
المشوار مكفّي: مفرق العدالة
الشفافية أساس وبلا أي محسوبية
ما في ولا تغطية
انلغت كل حصانة.
وصلنا لشارع المسؤولية
منّو ملعب رياضي
كل واحد عالتّاني بكب الطّابة
المسؤولية على الفريق، بس الغول إلي.
شارع النظام نده بالعالي
ما في ولا صف تاني
مش بس أنا مستعجل
بلا تفكير فردي خلونا نرجع للتفكير الجماعي.
شارع العلم والطبابة

بينده للكل انها حقوق أساسية
ما بينحرم حدا عبوابنا
لسّا ما صرنا تجاريّة.
شوارع كاملة للوظايف
شفافية تامة بلا أي واسطة أو عينونيّة
الكفاءة هي اللي بتحكي.
شارع الاستهلاك المسؤول
شعب واعي
سايكل الحياة منحترمو
الحياة مش واقفة بس عليي.
شارع السياسي بينده بالوطنية،
منا قصة زعامة حصانة أو مرتبة،
كل سياسي خادم لبلاده،
مش مهم سرايا أو عدد حراس المهم راحة وخدمة شعبه.
كل هالشوارع التقت على مستديرة القيم والايمان والمشاركة.
كلنا ايد وحدة ما بهم وين منطقتي،
الأهم انو المسؤولية مقسمة
كلنا مسؤولين عن بسمة بلادنا.

كتير حلوة كانت الكزدورة،

كنت حابب تدوم عطول

خلص الحلم وابتدا الكابوس

فقنا على دمار مرفأ بيروت،

الكابوس وعّانا من حلمنا،

حلم كل العمر رسمنا.

حلمنا نحس بالآمان بوطنا،

حلمنا نعيش مش بس كل يوم ننجا،

حلمنا بوطن يحضنّا،

كتير أجيال هاجرت غير حل ما كان في قدّامن.

هيدا الجيل عندو شمعة أمل،

قبل ما تدوب خلّونا سوا نحقّق كل أحلامنا...

الله يرحم الشهداء، ويشفي الجرحى، ويصبر شعبنا.

Beloved Lebanon

The journey started in the street of love,
a bright street
A street which doesn't recognize any
religious or political discrimination,
a street full of humanity.
The journey continues: Justice crossroad:
transparency is key and no favoritism,
no immunity,
preservation has no place here.
We're now in the responsibility street:
it's not a sports field,
We do not throw the responsibility ball at each other,
responsibility is on the team but the goal is for me.
System street screamed out loud:
no other line is allowed,

we're all in a hurry,
let's stop thinking as individuals and
start thinking as one community.
Education and medical services street
It claims to everyone that these are basic rights,
no one is deprived of them,
we're not commercial.
Streets providing all kinds of jobs,
complete transparency,
no need for a connection,
it's all about competency.
Responsible consumer street:
aware people, respecting life cycle,
knowing the world doesn't revolve around Me.
Political street claims patriotism,
it's not about getting a title nor favoritism,
every politician is a servant of the country,
palaces and bodyguards don't matter, what matters is serving the people.
A roundabout joins all these streets, a roundabout of values, faith and cooperation.
We're united, which area I come from doesn't matter,

what matters is a shared responsibility:
we're all responsible for our country.
The journey was fun.
I wish it lasted longer.
The dream has ended and a nightmare has started,
we woke up on Beirut port Blast
This nightmare stopped us from dreaming,
a dream I spent all my time imagining it coming true,
a dream of feeling safe in our own country,
a dream of living and not surviving,
a dream of a shelter.
Many generations have immigrated,
they have no other solutions
this generation still has a light of hope,
before it is gone, let us make our dreams come to life.
May the Lord have mercy on us.

The Meaning of Resilience

History! What is it? Why do you need to flip through the pages of history? And how to look at it? Earlier than now and before the explosion that happened at the port of Beirut on August 4, 2020, I was trying to run away from Lebanon's history.

Why to escape from it?

Because I was thinking that it would be hard to read and research about Lebanon without being empathetic with one party more than another. I was fearing to become the human I did not want to be. Until now, I do know a little about the history of the country and I do believe that a majority of citizens do know about it but only from one side of the story.

How does knowing history from one perspective affect us? Where does it lead to? How to create a book with the full history; complete canvas? Full, free from the lens of prejudice, while sharing all the facts and all the feelings?

The same incidence triggers different feelings for different parties. So what if we learn to listen to each other's feelings and pain, will that support us to rebuild the Lebanon we dreamed of for so long? Taking time to interact with different parties, listening to different stories, made me realize how strongly Lebanon is bleeding and how deep Lebanese's' wounds are. We are all in pain, our country has been bleeding for a long time now; from its earlier stage until now, it did not stop. Each new period has reminded that we are not taking time to be completely mindful of what our country is passing through. We are not acknowledging each other's pain, grief and sorrow.

What if we start doing so now?

Is it too late?

"Better late than never but never late is better. They tell me time is money, well we'll spend it together", Drake. So instead of continuing living fears alone as a small part of the bigger cocktail, why not spending time well, to create compassion, empathy, to create humans and not blind party members?

What happened in Beirut made me feel myriad emotions at the same time. Pain, fear, anger, disappointment, it made me lose hope at some moment and I just felt stuck, stuck like a spinning wheel in mud. But what if all of us lose hope, how will life look like then? Indeed, losing hope is never the best alternative.

Lebanon is and will always be a masterpiece. From natural beauty to cultural and religious diversity; a duty is to keep on drawing unity, real unity, not just slogans and words. Isn't it? Lebanon with all that he passed through is now becoming a role model to me, maybe to all of us. He is Becoming the meaning of resilience. He does always find the way to stay strong and keep moving forward, reconstruct, rebuild and thrive.

But how are we reshaping our dear country after each of the situations? Is it virtuous to keep on using the same strategy? A strategy of just putting dust under the carpet! Such approach has not worked so far, so will we keep on fearing the reality and discussing what is deep within?

This time let's try another strategy, let's think of building relations and humans before thinking of rebuilding the buildings and streets. Let's build a real Lebanese community, real active citizenship. Let's take the responsibility and act with compassion, empathy and curiosity. Let's learn how to listen! Let's learn to discuss while feeling rather than arguing. Let's learn to express respectfully with an intention of learning more and more from others, with the intention to break the ice and encourage others to express as well.

It is a new painful experience, but what is more painful is learning that now, more than ever people, especially youths, want to fly out without any will of returning. It is never a crime to travel seeking more expertise, knowledge and opportunity while saving your roots. Losing sight of your culture and history will just make your leaves turn pale, one after one. Then the day will come when your kids will remind you about your origin with so many questions of curiosity. What will you do then? How will you explain to your kids that it is important to never lose hope, to keep on trying, when earlier you did not? How will you explain the importance of taking care of the country when, at some point, you decided to turn a blind eye, without even looking back, without thinking of how to support it while being abroad? How will you share Lebanon's history, if you just have your own part of it and not the overall scenario? Where will all that lead to?

How ready are we to keep on living in the past? To keep on repeating history? For how long will we harbor the objective to have another nationality? How satisfying is that reality?

Foreigners wait summers and holidays to come and experience the beauty of Lebanon, while we just pass by all the grandeur with a lack of awareness. Lebanon certainly can be an example of conviviality if we want. He can be a destination for ecological, spiritual and cultural tourism. Lebanon can be a wellspring of new hopes and fulfilments. For all that to happen, we first need unity, we need commitment, we need accountability and transparency, we need patriots for the country. We need to be human and listen to each other deeply.

So, what is your role in reshaping Lebanon? What is preventing you from starting? What is the support that you may need? What are the challenges that you may face? How can you start from the reality you are in right now?

Think over it!

Each transition matters, get ready to experience and learn; transitions are what shape your current version.

"Allah sees you. He sees the hidden tears and fake smiles, He sees the pieces of your heart that has shattered. ask Him to heal you." Rumi

Introduction

Life is completely a journey: It starts with birth and ends at death and this is our physical life cycle; the one we are living right now. However, some believe that it all did not start just at our physical birth. Not at Physical birth! As they believe that, life was present even before birth. In that life, we were getting ready to step into our next transition. A Transition from spiritual life, to a physical one, but do we remember anything from the previous life? Not at all! At some point, we may feel that we have already lived that particular experience, what we call déjà vu. "I did the same but do not remember when? I have been through this scenario previously but I am not able to get the picture clearly," is what we remark. Maybe during all those moments, we feel connected to our previous life.

Who knows? Maybe one day we will get to know more about that previous life. But that moment, will not be now. That moment will transpire after another big transition. It will be after the so-called passing away. What will be there after passing away? No one has known the full picture. We just have some assumptions. In life, everything works in cycles. Even this life form we are living right now, is one of many transitions! We start as a spirit, a body is created and then back again to a spirit aspect. As Antoine Laurent de Lavoisier quoted "In nature, nothing is created, nothing is lost, everything changes". Therefore, it is all about transformation and transition.

This applies not only for humans but for nature as well, as we are part of it. From germination to becoming a tree, different transitions and transformations happen: trunk, branches, leaves, blossoms, fruits... This cycle is continuously repeating itself. This example showcases much more than the entire harmony of life! Let us take the example of a simple leaf, at some point it ejects from the tree and when it gravitates to the earth, it does not mean it is gone; that is just another transition. This leaf passes from a state of directly supporting the tree's life to nurturing the soil. This leaf stays there, but in another form, as Lavoisier mentioned, "here the leaf is not gone but rather transforming, just changing". When it was a leaf, its role was purely to nurture the tree and purify the air for us. However, as it kisses the ground, it becomes a natural fertilizer that supports the soil to be able to keep on its cycle.

So yes, many transitions are happening daily and with each new transition; a new purpose, a new role emerges. Now let us go back to our dear human. Oh yes! As life turns around them, what kind of transitions do humans experience? Are they just the someone at birth and the other ones at death? Do they have any other transition during their lifetime? Oh yes.

Like nature, trees, leaves... humans too pass through different transitional phases, so many that sometimes we do forget to celebrate them. The transitions happen in such a natural way that we do not feel them. At times, we just embrace them and welcome the new phase, for example getting married or becoming a father. Also, at some point, these transitions are so hard that they leave us with a wound. A wound that may take a lifetime to heal from. A wound that will be a part of our next transition, it will be part of us.

We may learn from it, or it may become a trauma, all these experiences are just what keeps a transition cycle going. Transitions are happening yearly, monthly, weekly, daily, hourly and even at each second that we live. Each new second brings a new experience, which makes a transition in our body, heart, mind and spirit. It will be really hard to walk you through the second-by-second transitions, but this book takes you on a journey of major self-transitions, while allowing you to dive deeper into your journey, your transitions.

CHAPTER ONE

Now

Where to start? Mmmm! Let us begin from where I am now; in a state of connection and harmony with life: a state of dancing with the flow: dancing with life, and what it has to bring as the next steps of the dance. I am not really good at dancing, I am impatient and sometimes resistant but I am trying to work on this. I am trying to work on myself more and more as there will always be a lot of work to do. There will always be new learnings, added values, new and old habits. It is not an easy process, yet an exciting one when we learn to embrace it.

So yes, a new transition makes you feel one with all that is around you. It makes you feel and experience the beauty of real life. It makes you enjoy the healing process of your previous traumas. Just like what is happening right now, with our dear Aunty Corona, it is a trauma for all of us. It is a challenge that has completely jammed our personal dance. It has interrupted all our plans and has taken us back to 'life dance', and what nature needs from us. Since a long time, nature has been trying to give us signs, anxious signs, without despairing, always trying to raise her voice: Climate change, seism, huge fires, tsunami and the list goes on.

She kept trying to attract our attention to where we are going. Unfortunately, few were able to listen, to listen carefully to her sorrow. She kept on sending signs till finding out that we are not able to connect with her, so then decided to deprive us from the freedom she gave us previously. She found out that we did not respect that freedom. We were too selfish while chasing our personal satisfactions, our personal desires. We focused too much on our freedom that we forgot that it is not only about freedom, rather about the 'full package'.

We sidestepped respect, responsibilities, contributions and we just focused on how to use the quoted "freedom" to reach our personal satisfaction level. Even if the price for that contentment was destruction, we still gave ourselves the right to make it happen, because it is our right to be free. It is our right to do whatever we want. Even if that led to selfishness, wars, destruction, environmental death, disrespect, dishonesty and impurity, yet we gave ourselves the right to be free. The right to be happy!

Freedom; what does it mean?

As per the definition, freedom is the state of not being imprisoned or enslaved, it is the power or right to act, speak or think as one wants. Unfortunately, too much of freedom had led us to be deprived of it. It has enslaved us in the cobweb of our acts and desires. But what about all humans around us? What about the entire system in which we live? What about life cycle? Did we really care about it?

Nature found out at the end of all her attempts the answer was NO! As we are not able to take a break ourselves, so nature has decided to impose it on us in her own way. In an instant, we found ourselves obliged to take a break, to breathe, and to reflect.

Here is another question: Are we aware of that nature's request to take a step back and reflect?

Let us now talk about it from another point of view, not from the angle of punishment, rather, from the perspective of healing. What did Corona try to stop us from? It tried to stop us from running behind the fully materialistic life. It stopped us from losing time looking for satisfaction, peace and harmony outside. It tried to make us realise that they need to be first found within to be able to harmoniously dance in life. Our inner self needs to be felt from the deepest soul and to feel it, connection is the key tool: connection within and connection with the outer world.

Corona is still trying to make us realize that we focus mostly on our own creations, our physical life, materialistic life, forgetting completely about the natural life, and natural life cycle. This has eventuated in the dearth of jobs; economies are just going down crazily. Why? Maybe to make us realize that economy had been created essentially to facilitate humans' interaction, not to use it as a tool of power and control, as it is used nowadays, maybe to make us realize that it is not the most important factor of life. It may be a secondary factor or even a completely unnecessary factor if used the way we do.

What did Corona do more? It supported natural healing, purifying air, cleaning water, regenerated greenery, freed up animals to enjoy what they were scared to do when we as humans were free. Nature did it not in our way but in its own natural way, in a way of respect, a way of connection. It took us back to the importance of home, not as a luxurious house, rather as a family, relations and support. However, this has not been an easy process due to emotional fluctuations; disagreements, conflicts and even violence are happening.

This gives us a message that we should not ill-use freedom. Freedom is respect!

We do all harbor the bubble of emotions. We all experience love, joy, happiness, stress, anger, disgust, fear and the list is too long. We do feel all of them depending on the circumstances and situations we are passing through. It is important to feel them, be aware of them, embrace all of them and also express them. In emotional intelligence, we call them self-awareness and self-management. We must know how to cope with these.

In positive leadership, we do differentiate between reacting and responding: Reacting means direct impulse, direct reply to our emotions felt in the moment. Whereas, responding is to take time to feel our emotions, understand them, cope with them to be able to find the best way to handle the situation. Responding is what leads us to social awareness and relation management to complete emotional intelligence factors. These are the aspects of feeling with others; being empathetic, feeling connected and work on creating better relations. All this together brings us back to what Corona is trying to teach us: Self-awareness, self-management, social awareness and relation management; the four highlights.

This time it's not only about emotions, rather it is about the overall life being aware of these four highlights, knowing what is important, and how to cope with it. It is about that bigger connection. Here, it is important to note that each action or response is a new transition leading to another reaction, affecting the overall system. How are we affecting our humanity? How are we affecting the overall system? How are our actions affecting our life?

Despite the fact of being spread worldwide in a hard time, thank you aunty Corona for the healing process and reflection time. Saying that I do feel peaceful, in harmony, and connected does not mean that I am perfect or an angel. It does not mean that everything is working perfectly either . I am still a human, I can make mistakes, still have unhealed wounds, and maybe some hidden traumas. I am a human, still experiencing the ups and downs, enthusiasm and depression. Dissatisfaction and struggles are what make our life exciting. It is always enthralling to overcome challenges, work on imperfections, and create solutions. Some may work out, others may be in the process and some may need to work out again.

Everything is connected, we are all passenger and at some point, we will be just a past memory, past story, an obsolete man or woman in the light of coming revolutions.

Serving life is a passion, enjoyable game of contribution. A hand can write, both hands can clap but more than that, the two can build. The more hands we have to create a better life, the more fruitful life will be.

So are you ready to roll up your sleeves? Are you ready to be connected to life? What can you do to feel that connection? What can you offer to life? What is your purpose? And how can we support each other?

We do have so many things in common. We do have so much work to do. We do have a mixture of talents, a toolkit of skills, and a special gift from our creator. A gift called mind. It is never too late to start, as the sooner we begin, the smaller will become the challenges. So let us start!

CHAPTER TWO
Career

Like any 24-year old, my major goal has been to build my career path. For that reason, I always looked for new opportunities. I graduated in 2013 and since then I found myself enveloped in the stress of finding a suitable job: what kind of a job do I want? Where can I find it? Also, how to find it? It was not easy, even now it is not easy. To give an overview, I was polyvalent. I have never worked longer than 9 months in a row for the same employer, so my financial security was not at its best.

While being a job seeker, I worked with my mother and brother in a small family business in order to stay active and steer-clear of the feeling that I am hopeless, useless or I do not contribute in the household expenses. The reason was simple: I followed the ideology "I need to give, to accept, to receive", in other words, "I need to contribute to be able to consume". Oh yes, it was not easy at all. The family business was seasonal as it was dependant on the annual academic schedule. Working months were 7 to 8 maximum, it was not easy at all, but I had unwavering faith in destiny. There was a point when I found myself drifting in the territory of depression. However, knowing my family, knowing the situation, I have always tried to build on enthusiasm, energy and positivity. I have always tried to keep my faith high. Yes, faith! In my mind, it was God who has a plan that I did not know. He was preparing me for what was coming. When He would find out that it is the best time, He will just open the next door, or show it to me while pointing at its key.

"But perhaps you hate a thing and it is good for you. And perhaps you love a thing and it is bad for you. Allah knows while you know not." (verse 216, Al-Baqarah of the Holy Quran).

This is mostly where I build my hopes. Sometimes, some friends or relatives kept on asking me, "Are you still applying? Do you think you will get a job? Don't you know how it works in our country?" I knew what they meant... Unfortunately, to get a job in a completely corrupted system, you must walk on the path of corruption. This is what they believed in. Yet, how come we have reached that level of slavery? That level of oppression! That level of submission!

At times, my mother said to me, "You know, if you continue this way, you will suffer in your life. You will be in huge pain, as you are walking against the river stream. At some point, you will be tired and the stream will take you. At that moment you will feel like a lost warrior, it will be too late for you."

I would often find myself ruminating over, "It is all about the train of life: Life is so speedy that maybe I will lose my seat ticket. Should I give up? Should I submit myself to corruption? But what about values? What about morals? What about that world that I dream of? Should I accept the bitter reality?"

Then, during those times of uncertainty, what was helpful was re-questioning my faith! As believing means accepting life. Feeling that higher connection, and being 100% aware of whatever is happening is for a reason. It may be hard to handle, but if it is happening, this means God has given you the strength to overcome it, or it is to make you stronger, it may even be one of the pillars enhancing your faith. It is a miracle, do not have any explanation of how and why?

But the more situations were becoming harder, the more my faith was taking the aspect of the zenith of any day. Zenith, yes at the peak of the day where the sun is perpendicular to earth and at the highest point. Like the highest zenith, my spirituality was at the zenith level as well. Just now while writing this analogy, I have realized why the zenith is the highest point of the sun and why it is perpendicular to the earth. Maybe, it is to reflect on our life. All the sun's steps and phases are needed for life, from sunrise to sunset. This phase has a mystery and harmony if observed. Just like life, any phase we tread through has its learnings, challenges and beauty. Yet, why Zenith, the highest point is perpendicular to earth?

In my opinion, the realization is that, to be at the zenith of our life, our vertical relation needs to be strong. We humans tend to focus on the horizontal relationship with life. We do focus on all that we can physically experience, touch, see, smell, listen or taste. So it comes back to our five senses, and we forget about an important sense, hidden in the corner. Hidden under all of that materialistic life, hidden in our deepest self. This sense is just our spiritual self. Having that said, our vertical relation is our relation with God, the creator, nature, the universe and ourselves. When that relation is at the zenith level, we feel lighter, in peace and harmony.

It is not always easy to reach this zenith. And mostly, it is not required to stay at that level, as to feel it fully, we also need to experience all the other steps. Any phase is needed to get the entire experience. Pain, suffering, darkness, anger, stress, failure, joy, happiness, success, peace, harmony… all such steps, emotions, situations are needed. However, just keep in mind what Martin Luther King said "Darkness cannot drive out darkness: only light can do that. Hate cannot drive out hate: only love can do that."

We will pass through all the aspects of life from sunrise to sunset, from light to darkness and at each step; we will be the only ones responsible for the outcomes.

In my hard darkened days, remembering the following was significant support "Oh you who have believed, seek help through patience and prayer. Indeed, Allah is with the patient." (verse 153, Al-Baqarah of the Holy Quran).

I was grateful to get some extra work, other than my family business or when I got the opportunity to work for a month or two in a conference center in Switzerland during the summer. It was a good source of revenue to keep going again within instability, as it was a short contract, but it was still better than nothing. What I was earning was enough to make me keep going until finding what was next. That also was a proof that God is in control, as the summer work was during the period of the closed family business.

Again, the temptation showed up after listening to the surrounding, temptation of corruption. Some called me crazy or illogical just because I let go some opportunities, opportunities of working with stability. I discarded those opportunities because in a direct or indirect way, I was required to submit myself to corruption to get them. What about the change? What about all the speeches on TV shows? Just hobbling bubbling. Just words with completely no actions, or actions contrary to the spoken words. Nevertheless, no, it needs sacrifices, it demands pain, and there are so many examples from history. God's messengers, for God did accept so many sufferings. Abraham, Youssef, Moses, Jesus, Mohamad (PBUT); the list is endless. They all passed through what I might be passing through and even through more. Some, because of the sake of God, did lose their entire family, friends, and life like the grandson of the prophet Mohamad (PBUH), during the so-called Karbala. Another example is Jesus Christ (PBUH), he did hold on to his cross, the humanity cross, for the sake of God.

Reflecting upon all those made me realize that, 'giving up' needs to be deleted from my dictionary, it needs to be omitted from anyone's personal dictionary. Let us take the example of a kid. When a kid tries to walk for the first time, he falls on the first step. If he decides to give up, fearing another fall, will he learn to walk? Will he enjoy the importance of walking? Will he know how helpful it is for him to walk? Similarly, what can you do that can support your growth? What can support you to keep on your track? As Gandhi said, "Be the change you want to see in the world", therefore, I have committed to myself to be that change as long as it is for the benefit of everyone even if I have to lose the self or lose my security and personal benefit.

You losing self-benefit in this world makes your spirit lighter and edge closer to the zenith. Finally, after 5 years of continuous search for a job, in 2018, I got my first job. Another new experience but here as well stability was a challenge as Social Worker's contract is for a few months, 6 months or a year. You never know for how long will you be able to avail that opportunity to serve while earning. You may receive an email at any time stating that you are needed for the human resources meeting. There could be a possibility that the email might come at the time of your promotion, changing position or non-renewal. In case of non–renewal, you have a month, two or three of notice period depending on how long you have served.

I was fearful of being fired anytime but then I thought why to water such fears, why to think so much. Living in stress of tomorrow, and at the same time losing the present. Let us make the best of what we have today; no one knows what will happen next. This is what Aunty Covid-19 has proved, she just jumped in and all our plans were cancelled.

So, my career was a mixture of my family business support, to hospitality and finally, I got into the social field. In each one of them, I discovered new skills, new relations, new connections. On the other hand, new challenges to overcome. I still remember some experiences were hard to handle. On a day, I was just nagging about the work situation and decided to share what I was experiencing and feeling with a close, trusted friend. That sentence, that answer he gave, I think it will just stay with me for the entire life. His reply was a questioning "Do you think you will find a job, work or company specially designed to fit in your values? You must reflect upon where you are, what can you bring. What difference can you make? Also, how to create the atmosphere you would like to be in? That was a turning point in my mind.

Wherever I will go, whatever I will be doing, there will always be challenges to overcome. I will never find a shoe that fits my feet perfectly. Adaptation may be needed. I may be in any corner of the world and can still experience that satisfaction, thinking that it is just a perfect life. Yet forming only perceptions may not work. In our life, we need to work on it. We need to create it. We need to do so in the place where we are actually.

If each one of us starts with small steps, considering where we are standing, it will just be perfect! It is not about position, the kind of work, or the working domain, it is more about mentality, spirit, perception and action. Anyone's contribution is just an added value. it is a mile in a marathon. We are all needed, and if you are a part of life on this planet, I do believe that it is, because you have a great role to play to create that perfection. The heaven that we talk about it is just our current life but on the spiritual level. It is just about complete harmony. Take an example of nature's harmony, how peaceful it is. Look at that complementarity, this is what creates nature's harmony. So, are we ready to complete each other? Are we ready to complete each other or do we prefer to keep on competing? What does it mean to complete each other? How to work on that complementarity?

CHAPTER THREE

Experience with Youth

Working with youth on the field was an objective. I do remember when I was asked, "Why have I chosen to start as a trainer?" The answer was, "To get to know more about youth, being present for them, listen to them and learn from their experiences, as each one has a personal story to share." It was not always easy, many times, I felt that I was failing but my hope for a better tomorrow always motivated me. A better future means to keep on trying with youth, even if they have been giving many reasons to give up. Society may not be supporting, therefore, the youth may lack motivation. They could be struggling, trying to find out a way to deal with uncertainty, inequality, and instability. After all, why to talk and discuss all those topics in a society where they are not needed anymore? Many first reactions were related to this question.

Communication, conflict resolution, negotiation, emotions, citizenship, responsibility, being assertive rather than passive or aggressive... Will we really need them? How can these skills support us in finding jobs? After all, the major objective of the majority of youth is to find a job to survive in the coming days. Some others join the training just to have a space of escape from life's reality, life pressure, just to have a new small breath.

There was a time when I felt that I was not skilled enough, I questioned myself about my ability to create connection and space to grow together. Within groups of 20 to 25 youth or more, it was not easy to stop the session and try to have a one-to-one discussion to find out what is not working out, and what are the personal challenges each one of the participants are passing through. After the session, it was not always possible as well to have a one to one discussion with the participants as the bus driver was already there and waiting to take them back home. Moreover, the phone number given by participants was mostly the number of one of their relatives, so during working hour it was hard to reach the participants by phone.

Feeling powerless, was at some point, energy-draining. The energy gets a boost when some participants reach out and share their own experiences and how the sessions are supporting them in daily life. For example, I remember the day when after one of the sessions, I found a paper on the windshield of my car. The paper read 'thank you for the sessions, they are a support'. Or on other occasions, when my colleagues go for a focus group discussion and some great feedbacks are shared, and here again, the energy level goes high. This amplifies the enthusiasm to keep going even if it is challenging.

At the same time, there is a discussion with a lot of disagreement when we talk about conflict resolution. We live in a society where the use of power is a rule. Where it is considered as being strong, being assertive expressing disagreement without violence is considered as not possible. If you do it that way, others will see you as weak and vulnerable. How easy it is to react and opt for violence, at the same time how deep will be the wounds of that violence?

"Nonviolence doesn't always work -- but violence never does", Isaac and Asimov.

Violence is never a solution, it leads to more tension and violence, yet it is most common in practice. I am not saying that I am always peaceful, unfortunately, sometimes, my reactions are strong and maybe violent. Violence can be using a certain power, or even using words that will harm the other person. Being non-violent does not mean not to share your disagreement or emotions, it means channelizing your emotions to be shared in a healthier way.

One of my sessions was about the difference between reacting and responding, continuous awareness is needed. In each circumstance, we will need to react or respond, what worked during a previous incident may not work for the new one. It is not easy but how beautiful will our life and the world be without all that violence? How will it be with less violence? A part of the program was to pass on the responsibility to youth. Let them create their own social initiatives, become leaders and implementers. That step as well was not always simple. Youth who are struggling on a personal level, being active in society was not a priority for them. Personal responsibility is a missing ingredient; they were not feeling to be a part of the society. No one will listen to us! We cannot change anything! The entire system is wrong; it is not possible to do anything about it! This was all that was shared during each brainstorming session.

Nowadays, it is easier to go for a shisha , a day in the game of PUBG, to escape from the feeling of inability, than working on transforming our own capacities. It is the way life has been shaped now; lying on our sofa, eating, drinking, smoking, behind a screen, having a fake social life, and we let life the way it is. Who knows maybe at some point, we will even stop using our brain and mind and just behave like robots. How can our life change if we keep on living the same way? How to expect new achievements with same repeated actions?

Complaining without action! Complain and not taking our own part of responsibility in hand! Complain and just follow the crowd, is that the way to shape our future that we believe in? It was maybe hard to create responsibility, motivation, and leadership, but what was magical was to see sparkles in youth's eyes during the initial implementation. Some of the youth were leaders by nature, which gave hope. Leaders needing an opportunity to be responsible. During one of the implementations, I do remember that they took a whole responsibility. When challenges happened, they did find how to overcome them with their own motivation and high commitment. They were living the moment, becoming leaders, shaping a project that they drew from A to Z. It was their project, their own masterpiece. Those were the days of hope, days of rebirth. For how long will those days stay? For how long will the energy level remain high? No one knows.

The objective was to create sustainable initiatives, sometimes we do check with some youth but it is not always easy to check with all. The highest level of joy is created when youth themselves come back to us with great news about their ongoing active contribution. After all, the shared skills must stay with youths, the purpose behind such training is to create active citizens rather than passive human, to reshape the society.

This generation is prone to so many challenges, obstacles, wars, division and competition, how to create unity and hope? Create hope not for a small moment but hope for a better life. How to give them credit, to make them a key component of shaping the future? After all, hope is what shapes our life, no hope means no life. "Hope can be a powerful force. Maybe there's no actual magic in it, but when you know what you hope for most and hold it like a light within you, you can make things happen, almost like magic." – Laini Taylor.

It was easy to observe those youths, criticizing or judging them, but when listening to some of their deep stories, respect sprouted. Life hasn't been simple for majority of them, it has been challenging and full of wounds. So, listening deeply to their stories will be enriching for sure. They may add so many chapters to the encyclopedia of life. They are young but they have experiences to share. What they need is to have space, to have people willing to listen, listen; not to judge, listen and feel with them. Life's recipe needs all of us, all of our stories, all our experiences. Each one needs to celebrate life and always work on creating an updated self-version.

After all, life is in continuous change like any product. After our maturity, the quality of our life may decline and keep on declining; or we may choose to create an extension. After that extension, again we may have a choice to allow a new decline or another extension. It is the same process with each one of us, do we want to stay stagnant on a certain self-version? Do we want to keep on declining? Or do we always want to keep it on with a new extension for a better self? What can support us in creating a better self? How to keep on going?

Another personal challenge was about targets. It was about quantity, about numbers and obligations. During some phases, the target pressure does step in. At the end of the year, the quality of the services delivered is hard to measure, what can be measured is numbers. The number of youth attending, here it was a personal dilemma focusing just on the target, it was not the purpose. For me, it is not about numbers; it is about humans, stories, complete entities, it is about dignity, rights and compassion.

In those phases, a lot of personal efforts were needed to be able to handle target and project goals, cope with stress while giving always the best of quality service. Is really the quantity important? What about quality? Do we have to focus on the dimension of the land? Or do we have to focus on the seed's values? Should we focus only on the quantity harvested? Or should we focus as well on nutriments in each harvested fruit?

"We don't value craftsmanship anymore! All we value is ruthless efficiency, and I say we deny our own humanity that way! Without an appreciation for grace and beauty, there's no pleasure in creating things and no pleasure in having them! Our lives are made drearier, rather than richer! How can a person take pride in his work when skill and care are considered luxuries! We're not machines! We have a human need for craftsmanship!" Bill Watterson

There's Treasure Everywhere. When done each thing with passion, it becomes a masterpiece. Passion is really what is needed in education, when going to a session, classroom or workshop. It is important to know that your attitude, behaviour and responses have the same importance as the curriculum. In our current education system, we need to focus more on having educators than having just skilled teachers. What remains with each student is the educator's attitude and not the quantity of chapters delivered.

I very well remember one of my university lecturers, not because of the course content, but for his attitude and life's philosophy. After my graduation, I decided to search for his contact to learn more and hear more from him. It was not easy to do as he is not much active on social media.

When I found him on LinkedIn, it was a great pleasure to connect to him. Then we scheduled a meeting, and the time passed with him was really quality time. Not about university lessons, but about life experience and perception.

"Value is what to sell, Quality is what to say, and quantity will automatically fall in." Aisha S. Kingu.

To give meaning to life, we need to value each of its components. We need to give fully, being fully present and aware. Whatever we are offering, offer it freely and fully. This is not always easy, yet this is the only way to transcend. Some of the participants I had the pleasure to partner with are now my friends, they are transcending in their own paths. This gives me utmost happiness. When I was young, I always said that I will never be a teacher, but today, I am working as a life skills trainer and facilitator. Now I feel that each person sharing knowledge, skills or creating spaces for people around to express is a blessing, especially when given with compassion and passion. So, how is your life journey so far? How can you move to your next transcendent level? What can you offer with passion?

CHAPTER FOUR
India

To go or not to go was the question here. It was in 2018 when I got that excellent opportunity to work. It was an external work with a monthly salary and health insurance. Even if it was on the contracting level, a short-term contract, but still it was a good beginning. It was a beginning to work on plans that had been put on hold for so long, I had been postponing many plans.

I was satisfied with the training I was delivering, enjoying what I was doing. Yet, I felt something was missing, I was looking for more impact, more contribution, it was not enough for me. I wanted to give more, and I knew I could give more. An Idea was provoking me for long. Since my first attempt to go to India, it was like a calling, like a destiny to go there.

Before starting my job, I did try again to make it to India, there was some complication with the visa process as rules and procedures changed months before I had applied. At that moment I was applying as an intern for a program at Asia Plateau, it was to go deeper in training I had completed previously at Caux with a movement called Initiatives and Change (IofC). India and Switzerland are the two biggest centers of the movement. In both centers , programs and conferences happen yearly. The new rule stated that to be able to go as an intern, I should be a fresh graduate or still studying, and guess what? I was a graduate since 2013, so not that fresh as it had been 5 years.

For the second time, God did not want me to go, for sure for reasons. Later, I found out that it was because He was preparing me for a new job experience. He always protects you and holds you back until the right time comes, what is needed is trust and faith. Still, the idea of going to India was pressing upon me. To go or not to go, that was the question that prevailed for around 3 months. What supported me to take the decision was maybe the lack of surety if the project will be renewed. The managers were still working on it. Therefore, around a month before the term of my contract, I decided to write an email to the concerned human resource. It was to check if there was any update regarding my working position.

In that email, I was honest and shared that I had an opportunity to go to India for a great experience that may support my growth. So at that moment, the HR was comprehensive, and just said that they will make their best to work on renewing the project by October, but nothing was sure. She ended the email by asking me about my motives. At that point, I just decided that if I do not take this opportunity now, the idea will hunt me for my entire life.

So I decided to make it happen; to go to India at the end of the actual contract. I expressed that it will be a pleasure to collaborate once again, when I will be back from India in case the project in renewed. What changed the scenario in my favour was just some invitation letters from friends, which made me eligible for a visa. What a crazy step that was, but I had to do it.

Finally, it was time to make it, to listen to that voice. To be honest, while landing at the airport of Mumbai, I noticed saying to myself, "what have I done?" I wanted a one-year visa but I was about to land in Mumbai on a three-month visa. Then I said to myself "I should not regret, I cannot go backward, so to make the best of this experience, I need to live each moment fully". It turned out to be an amazingly, enriching experience. It was not always that easy, but friends and team members made it smooth and unforgettable.

The first week was peaceful at the centre, just chill with some service support. Then came the day when the real journey began. It was time to go to Pune from Panchgani, then take a night flight with my teammate in direction of the North-East, Nagaland. There was a stop at Pune for a few hours before the next flight. So, I met a friend at Pune. He welcomed me so warmly. In fact, he was a friend of friends (from the IofC family of friends). Within first few seconds, we became close friends. We did not take much to connect and go into deep conversation, just IofC charming spirit . He invited me to a great Indian diner and asked me what would I want to do during that free time before my flight. So we decided to go to a nearby temple and just have time to connect and discuss. Hours flew by in the wink of an eye and then it was time to go back to the airport.

Let the journey begin. It was a long travel, national flight, car, and toktok so many transportation transitions. It was exhausting and then I reached the house of Listening "Kerünyü Ki", an open house that always welcomes IofC friends and takes care of them. A warm shower was necessary to relax the muscles. The story of the house, Uncle and Aunty, it was all like a fairy-tale. It was a real life in community; each one contributing, supporting and sharing tasks. It was followed by an introduction to the team, reflection time, listening to plans, and getting ready physically, spiritually and mentally.

The first Intervention, first delivered program was at Mokokchung. We were going to pass on IofC values, to teachers or to-be teachers, pass on the importance of reflection time, the importance of taking responsibilities of change, starting from personal change. It was a two-day program, each day with a new group of 60 participants. For me it was the first time that I was standing, delivering a session to more than 30 participants first, and second to experienced teachers. I would take a deep breath before the session, took some time to get ready, and then just danced with the flow.

The participants were so receptive but at the same time, their contribution was making our Dal soup tastier. Here Dal soup refers to our session, as it was an analogy done at the beginning, which made it tasty with the diversity of ingredients. As well, from place to place, the taste has the same essence but different, just like our session. To make it rich and enjoyable, everyone's contribution, sharing and experience were needed.

On the second day, we concluded the session in a special way. We discussed about the world, our responsibilities! How do we want our world to be, and then decided to end it with a group prayer. We stood up, held our hands to form a circle and prayed for the world for a few minutes, we prayed for more unity, peace, equality; and equity. For few minutes, I felt the overall shared energy, I felt like I was flottering over the world's surface.

A fact that attracted my attention was the hospitality of our host. To make our program happen, the host and some associates had contributed a sum of amount to be able to take care of all our expenses, food and accommodation. Even on the last day, our host took us for a tour. Visiting the place was just soul-invading. Greenery, nature, culture and I remember the story of two lovers like Romeo and Juliette with a tragic end. Two towers had been built, facing each other, symbolizing their love, and inability to be together. It was the story of Jina and Etiben. While narrating the story, I could feel the wave of pain in the words of the host.

They really felt the need for such a program, and for that they did all they could do to make it happen. Our dinner time was always together in the house of one of them. The food served was cooked with so much love that it was hard to resist to take a second serving and sometimes a third. Someone shared that "in our culture if there is no second serving, it means you did not like the food, so it will be offending", but naturally, the food was lovingly tasty. I was happily going for a second run. Over meals, small discussions would happen and then back to the allocated hostel to sleep. Our last night was a complete chill.

The next day, we had to wake up early to take the road back for another journey. Yet, we stayed longer around the bonfire, musical time, talents, songs in different languages, small culture sharing. It did not end here, it was surprising and warm to notice that our hosts and school principal came early in the morning to the station, and they gave us a bag with snacks for the road travel.

Again, it simply highlighted all the lovely care they provided to us. It was like the cherry on the top of a cake . After that, we went to several places to deliver sessions, have dialogues and conferences and at some places, we just spent a night or two just as transit . Some audience were more than a group of 100 in a session and there were smaller groups as well. A 5-day dialogue conference was also planned, organised and implemented. It was astonishing to feel welcomed everywhere we went. The IofC fellowship web. There was always someone to take care of us, as the host or to arrange things for us.

Even when our programs were delivered with our IofC friends from the same region, at some points they were taking care of our accommodation. India is so vast, and IofC fellowship web as well. Generosity, contribution, service, community is always in their mind. How to not be willing to give yourself fully, give all what you can in such a bubble of solidarity?

At some point, flexibility and adaptation were really needed due to space, the number of participants, or even changing plans. I do remember one of the interventions had to be reshaped completely a few minutes before the agreed time. We were supposed to deliver a 3-hour session for 30 to 60 participants, and we got a last-minute notice on the spot that the time was reduced to 1 hour. We had to complete our session within this time while addressing all the students of the school in the Court. A small meeting, prioritization, what is the most important to deliver, and let it be.

Being with the outreach team was a learning experience on a daily basis. The material was the same, but each one had a personal way of delivery. Each one in the outreach team has his own stories of changes, struggles and challenges. Sharing our stories just made our bond even stronger on the human level, we were more than just teammates for a few months. The bonding was so strong that we felt none of us tried to dominate as there is at least one dominator in a team. On a day, one of my outreach friends asked me "Did you go for your morning run?" I replied "No, why?" "Just because your energy level is not as usual, maybe you need a run!" They knew from previous sharing, that physical activity is important for me, so the question was to bring this to my awareness. The day after, I was ready to run. How important it is to reach that level of connection, in our relations.

I feel grateful for being a part of the outreach team maybe for just few days, yet learnings, and experiences will always stay within me. It was a Golden opportunity and thanks for each one who contributed in making it unforgettable. I do remember one day when we were in a state all of us were unfamiliar to. Help was needed, whom to ask about the information to get to our destination. The woman we asked gave directions on where to go to get public transportation toward our destination. Then, when she realized that, we were all outsiders; she walked back with us, stopped public Toktok, and bargained the price. What an action of care it is! Her intention was just to ensure that we reach our destination easily and that we pay a reasonable price for it. What a blessing, what a caring attitude she had. So many instance, so many stories, each new day was a new learning.

One of the direct feedbacks received while delivering sessions, was "the first impression as a team working together was the image of unity". We were a mix cultural team, from different parts of India, Tibet, Nepal, China and Lebanon. Building Unity in a Divided World was our vision. Something that retained my attention was the fact that India is the first country in the world to make corporate social responsibility (CSR) mandatory. Making investors, support social work, support the society and local communities. At several, places, we found ourselves receiving donations for the movement, knowing that what we were doing was completely a volunteering work. It was a way to say that "we support what you are doing, and we are aware of its need".

Siloam Center was one of the destinations. There we held a 5-day dialogue. In parallel was happening a youth program as well. Students from a certain School had a program and a social project. The project was to support during Christmas day, in organizing and implementing, a yearly event happening at the center. On that day, the Center was opened for the public, all kids from the nearby localities came to enjoy, play, participate in activities, win gifts, and have food for free. It was just AWESOME to see all the shared joy. Here as well, it is important to highlight a small point, in studying curriculum it was mandatory to make a social contribution. This again highlights the importance of personal contribution toward a better society. How impactful it will be when done freely, not because of grade, rules, or any obligation?

"It is not about how much you do, but how much love you put into what you do that count", Mother Teresa. Multi-Faith prayer! Have you ever heard about it? It was just magical, like just right now while talking about it I am feeling thrills. As part of the dialogue, we had a mutli-faith prayer time. Setting was ready, round table in the middle, some candles and flowers, chairs around the table, little of soft music before prayers started. It was a time wherein each one could pray in his/her own dialect, according to own belief. It was a space to connect us spiritually despite our differences. It was like feeling connected to serenity. From that experience, I can hold with me the importance of real relationship, teamwork, resilience, flexibility, adaptation, care, service and most importantly; simplicity. Simplicity to find real joy and happiness.

I still remember that little girl full of joy and energy. A girl that I was just happy to observe while she was teaching her small brother. Her enthusiasm just made the atmosphere full of willingness to learn. I do pray for her as she deserves to be an impactful future leader.

Another intense experience was observing parents, kids coming to a public source of water, to draw some water to take back home. Coming from a place where water is just steps far away, using infrastructure and tape, I should be grateful more often, for all what I do have. Being grateful is not enough, we also need to work on reducing our over consumption and waste. Waste of food, waste of water, waste of time, waste of resources, and just share the excess. Sharing is an important, factor as we all know "sharing is caring". A quote about poverty and sharing of Mother Teresa is really interesting, "Poverty is not made by God, it is created by you and me when we don't share what we have". What are you grateful for? What is your part of responsibility in reducing waste? What can prevent you from sharing?

CHAPTER FIVE

First Travel Alone

It was June 2013, my graduation time. At that point was thinking that it was the time of making big achievements. I will get a good job, feel secure, stable and had just starting realizing my dream of having my own family. Family house, with a partner that I cherish and kids running around. Plans and dreams were snowballing. I knew it important is to dream and keep dreaming, or losing hope will be easy. But, plans do not always work as set. And yes, none of my plans worked out at that period, so I decided to delay the dream deadline.

If I remember well it was February 2013, a friend shared a link with me about an international program held in Switzerland. That program was scheduled in the summer and I was not able to apply as that was our exam period. I got to know about the program a few days before the deadline. At that moment, my priority was my exams. Another reason was that if I apply, I will need to read the entire application, check the website and do researches first. I still took out time to discover more about the movement. It was a movement about change, responsibilities, peace, leadership, dialogue, personal change, contribution, morals, values; it was just too big.

This program played in my mind till 2015 but due to personal instability, was not able to take that step. I was still not working, not financially independent. I do not recall how I got to know that the same program delivered at Caux, in Switzerland is also held in India as well at Asia Plateau. The only difference was that in Switzerland, it was of about four weeks and in India for about six months.

A small or may be a huge difference but still worth to make it. That opportunity of going to India, made me remember my time in high school when one of my friends always said to me "you know, you need to find out an Indian future spouse, there are so beautiful". So yes, I said I do not have anything to lose; it may be a great experience.

I started ruminating deeply about the program, like how to make it? No work! Then I decided to talk about it to my family and tried to highlight, the positive points of making it saying that we never know it may open other opportunities for me. So they accepted to support me on that. I started working on my visa process, all was going well; each new day bringing closer to the travel day and was increasing my level of enthusiasm. I received a call, to go and collect my visa. I was finally peaceful that there was nothing that may prevent my new experience to happen. Guess what? I was completely wrong! All was ready, planned scheduled, but you can never be 100% sure unless it happens. This time it did not!

Circumstances, life, events, external factors may always put any plan on hold or completely cancel it at any time. That was the case, due to another family priority; my travel to India had to be cancelled. This travel was planned from late 2014 to Early 2015. Then, as always, God has a certain plan, I did receive a link to apply to. It was the link to the same program happening in Switzerland, yes again. This time in the summer of 2015. So I decided to apply. At that moment, I was just completely in disequilibrium, I was a graduate since last two years but still no work. Along with being unemployed, knowing that if the inactivity period will be long, it becomes harder to find a job. You may know well the so-called "what experiences do you have while applying as a fresh graduate?".

At that moment, I thought about the great experience! Switzerland! Conference center! Possibility of a new working opportunity! This year many things were turning on. I did two short internships, and also applied to pursue studies in France. So many happening at the same moment. I also got accepted in France at Lille for a Master's in Business and international relations.

Before buying the plane ticket, I was asked, "As you are accepted to pursue your studies, are you sure you still want to go to that program." The program was known as the Caux Internship Program, now known as the Caux Peace and Leadership Program. And I said yes as I did not want to lose that opportunity. Finally, I was about to discover what destiny had in store for me. What will I discover there?

After around two years of trials. In mid-June, it was time to fly, to a new unknown. A completely new experience, it was the first time when I was traveling alone. Reaching a new country, not knowing anyone there. Still, I was lucky as I speak French, so it was easy for me to communicate. It was a travel divided into small travels. After the program in Switzerland, plans were to come to France to spend some time with my relatives there and check a place to stay for my master's studies.

So, the first transit was in France, where I stayed for a day in a family friend's house before boarding a train to Geneva. Being welcomed to the house and introduced to the family was the first step. The hospitality and support were just heart-touching. This Family did not know me from before, they knew my sister and her husband. The way this man supported me, even while not really knowing me, was just amazing. Let me highlight here the importance of support. That Support, in an unknown place and going to another unknown place made me feel comfortable and at peace. He just prepared everything for me, train ticket, room to stay at for the night, picking me up from the airport knowing that he was on a working day, and dropping me to the train station the next morning. Everything was prepared to make me feel welcomed and supported. We spent just a few hours together, but it was enough to feel connected and grateful.

Important are the relationships that are not because of any interest, but just to cherish. Like this man who supported me unconditionally, with no agenda at the back. Since then I believe that I saw him again just once, but we are still in good contact.

So I woke up early, as usual, I did the morning prayer, took the shower and got ready to leave. He gave me all the directions and requested me to call as soon as I reach the center. From France to Geneva, then from Geneva to Vevey, Vevey to Montreux and finally Montreux to Caux. While I was in the train from Montreux to Caux, I remember that I was amazed by the landscape, nature and beauty. Amazed, at the same time stressed about the experience, thinking of what was waiting for me there. It was my first international experience. It was the first time I was going to pass a full month out of home, far from my family. It was the first time I was going to share room with strangers. Then I decided to take a deep breath and just relax.

I looked around and found a group of three youths, discussing, mostly in Spanish. Luckily I had got the opportunity to learn Spanish earlier so I was able to understand their conversation to an extent. When we are familiar with any language, we tend to speak easily and fast. For me who did not have the opportunity to practice, it was not that easy to get all that was being said. I do not remember what started our conversation. How did it start was not really important, but started with an introduction and found that we are going to the same place. Two of them had enrolled in the same program. How amazing it was! A few minutes back they were strangers, now teammates.

We continued discussing, discovering each other. Normal, general, introduction. Who are you? From Where? What do you do in life? How did you know about the program? And things like that. From time-to-time, we also took breaks to enjoy the view and capture some pictures. As I said earlier, it was just a beauty, going up the hill, in that small train, taking altitude and looking down to the lac. Lac Leman was enough with light blue to take you into a journey of reflection. Adding to that, greenery of the trees, dense vegetation, and sunny windy day. Altogether, just natural harmony. It was breath-taking, just silence and observation. What an unexpected introduction to the unknown! "Caux station, can you see it?" Finally, we are there! We needed to take our luggage. As we stepped down the train, we were warmly welcomed by some strangers who were going to become known in the next few seconds. They were team coordinator members. They took us to the palace, to the reception and find out how we were allocated; Floor and room number then we dispersed, each one went with one of the team members to be directed to the rooms while getting information about mealtime and so on.

In the elevator, I was with this new stranger, and it turned out that he did speak Arabic; it made me feel comfortable, as it was not that easy for me to speak English fluently at that time. I felt calm and connected while discussing, I came to know that he was also from Lebanon, my native country. He took me to my room, informed me about the meeting point and time for the next meal. Then he left, allowing me to get more familiar with the room, the place and to rest after that long journey. What an amazing coincidence! Teammates in the train! A splendid place for reflection! Warm Welcome! Arabic speaker, Lebanese team member! What more was needed to feel comfortable, at peace, safe and in harmony! From that moment, fear was completely erased and replaced by curiosity, enthusiasm and willingness to grow. How do you feel before any new experience? How can fear affect your full experience? What can support you creating the best out of each new experience?

CHAPTER SIX

CPLP

On the break day, as I reached the center a day in advance due to flight unavailability, I got the opportunity to feel familiar with the place, space, and people were already there. I do remember, on the next morning meeting, we were requested to join. I did, and it made me feel included. Then at the end of the meeting, the responsible senior member of our program approached me to have a discussion and asked me "What do you like to do in your free time usually?" I just said cooking. She asked me if would you like to be in the kitchen team during your service time, and I said yes with pleasure.

In fact, the program was divided into training, courses and service time to feel a part of the community, to support in the center's activities. Ultimately, it was the day. First day was the introduction and induction day. Finally, I got to know about other participants. We were more than 30, from different backgrounds, cultures countries, from around 20 different countries. In the beginning, it was hard to remember names but with time, we got familiar with each other. I do remember well our two trainers; one was a bubble of energy, optimism and enthusiasm; and the other more into calm, peacefulness and care.

The program was basically based on reflection, and inner digging. This aspect made all the difference. Others programs and trainings were more informative and idea-driven. This one had the smallest part informative and the rest interactive and reflection. One of the activities experienced on the second or third day was on trust building. We were still unacquainted to each other, and were divided to two groups. I was in the first half, the group of blindfolded, not knowing what was happening. Just sitting, in a room, with some thoughts which starting raising a pinch of stress and anxiety.

What is happening? What that moment in emptiness? What is going to happen in a few moments? What will the facilitator request us to do? Suddenly, I felt someone catching my arm. I just resisted, refusing to move. Who is that persons, why me? So many other questions surfaced in my mind. I tried to speak to the person without any answer. It took maybe a minute or a little more to accept the idea that I should move. Why? After all those questioning, in my mind I reached the point that we were here for a program, so we are in a safe space, and no one will harm us. Then I decided to move and went through the path with an unknown guide. Trust! What does it mean? Is it really important in our society and the current corrupted system? All those conflicts around! Mmmmm how to talk about trust? Do not just talk about it, you need to work on it. As the first step, you need to trust yourself, be confident, and understanding that it will not be that easy to create. What does trust mean to you? And how can it be created?

With all that division, all that violence, all that self-centred mind, it will be hard to create trust. Trust once lost is hard to rebuild, it was one of the Remarque during my business course. It is important to work on preserving the current client. Work on loyalty, and if at any time, a client loses trust, it is hard or may be impossible to gain it back. If it is so hard to regain trust in case of business and clients, what about places where the similarity between divided humans is pain, suffering and blood? What about people who lost their beloved? What about those who even saw how their friends and brothers were killed? What about all those kids that now need to live without parents? But on the other side, how will be life in the coming few years? In 10 years? 20 years? How will it be if distrust keeps on growing? Do you think we will enjoy life then? Will it be enjoyable to live an entire life of fear?

In that program, the discussion was about forgiveness. Oula! What a tuff topic! It was not only about speeches, talks and words. It was real stories of forgiveness. Stories from around the world, like the story of Irène Laure, the Imam and the Pastor and so many others. Stories of reconciliation, stories of forgiveness. Forgiveness a hard process, yet the magical part was each one experiencing it was just expressing how lighter personal life became. After each session, we were having personal time to reflect on what just happened, and the topic and discussion. Sometimes, it was hard just after the session to forget all what we discussed. Reflection went with us to rooms, and then with us back home. Even until now, that reflection is with me. It has become a habit, a life style.

During the program, for a full month when it was time to reflect, instead of writing down on paper my thoughts, I was just sketching and drawing. Within myself was saying, I have not travelled this far to write down my thoughts. So many topics unfurled, so many discussions. Discussion during sessions, during meals, during outings; each day was to cherish with a full potential of discovery. What about my service time? It was always with pleasure to go to my service shift. Chefs were just so warm. Even the early morning shift was a pleasure. One of the learnings from one of the chefs was "When you start a task, do not go to another one before finishing the first one" and "don't run in the kitchen", whatever has to be done, do it peacefully. If you run, you may do more harm than achievements.

Remember "Good things come slow, especially in distance running." Bill Dellinger. My service shift was alternating two days in kitchen and one day in the buffet zone. There, in the buffet area or even early morning, the forum director of the centre was always happy to support and serve when needed. He was just doing it with so much love that you just have the impression that he is on a dancing platform. Yes! He was the Forum center Director, and coming to serve. In house there were no titles, we were all equal. We all did serve each other. Any conference participant as well was having community service time to support us.

This is the world that we want to create, a world of trust, equality and service. A world where we do not see others as tittles, positions, social rank, caste, we see others just as humans. It was just so astonishing in the beginning when you have community support in your team, a certain ambassador, mayor, teacher, engineer, farmer; everyone serving with pleasure. To make our life better, we must serve. We must serve each other; we need to serve life. We are life's servants.

We were in the mid-way of the program when we experienced a hike. It was not a simple hike; it was the hike to enjoy the sunrise from the top of the mountain. For that reason, we needed to get ready and move by 2:00 am. We were in Ramadan, I was fasting and for me, that was a personal challenge to wake up at 2:00 am while holding on to my fasting. Spirit high, energy charged, mind ready so let us go. It was just a dark, and cold night, majority of the team joined the hike. We were following each other, at this time I decided to stay at the back. The beginning was kind of smooth, we passed by some cars, and we were still nearby some houses. It was like a normal walk. However, as we stepped into the woods, the track became harder and some were on the point of giving up. That was where trust was needed. We were supporting each other, holding our hands, pushing our limits, supporting personal trust, as well as trusting each other. That feeling at the top, the feeling of achievement, was not that of a personal challenge completed, but much more as all of us did it, we reached at the top together.

How amazing will life be if we all follow the same approach! Collective life, not just me, not just you, but 'we' on the top.

After we reached the top, it was time to celebrate, some hugs, some snacks, reflection with a beautiful sunrise, we did not forget to take pictures. The way down was much easier, smoother, full of light, the sun was already with us. We were able to stay as long as we wanted on the top, I preferred to not stay for long so that I could take some rest before my service time.

Yes! That is life, you may decide to make yourself happy, but always keep in mind that there are duties and responsibilities to respect. That hike made me realize that nothing is impossible as long as there is a will. It made me realize that life's path will never be easy, there will always be challenges to overcome, some may be easy and other harder, and all of them are what add flavor to life. This is what makes us celebrate and feel the impact of our achievements. It also made me realize that achievement, like anything else in life, is more powerful when it is collective rather than individual. When you have that will, power, or strength, it does not mean that you run alone or make others feel weak. It means that your responsibility and duty, is to be present, be ready to support others. It makes you feel that you should steer-clear of self-interest and supporting only your own growth. Support others to overcome their own challenges, understand them and keep in mind that they may need more time than you to advance. If they are slow, give them a helping hand, if they fall, be ready to support and support the healing process.

"It is better to go slow in the right direction than to go fast in the wrong direction" Simon Sinek. It is better to grow as a team than running individually, hurting or trampled on others. As there is an African proverb "If you want to go fast, go alone, if you want to go far, go together".

It was my first international travel, my first alone travel, an experience full of reflections, learnings and connections. Since that moment I felt the importance of confidence while staying humble. The importance of not always following, or staying passive, feeling depressed. It is important to stand for what you believe in, especially when it is not for your own interest, when it is to reshape the world into a better place and to be passed on to the coming generation. Sometimes you need to take a lead, you need to take the initiative, it may be a small or big step, but it will be the first step towards your biggest dream. What is your dream? What actions are needed to make it happen? What support do you need? What lead can you take?

CHAPTER SEVEN

Way Back

Days passed so fast, in a wink and it was the end. As the program concluded, we celebrated it, and received our certificates. It was the night when we started thinking how would life be from the next day. We knew it, at some point or another it will be the end of such an enriching experience. We knew that our life would not be the same anymore. It will be the time to move on to a new transition, to a new aspect of life.

The one who is born today will take an exit from this world someday. When is that specific time? No one knows! What we know is that it will happen and it can be at any time. We may be at the beginning, midway or end of our purpose, yet it will happen.

On that last evening of the program, sleeping early was not possible. It was our last time together, and still some more messages to write. In the early morning, the program ritual started. It was a continuous trajectory to the train station. Hourly, or every two hours of goodbyes farewells, tears and emotions rolled. Within, it was a mixture of emotions, a boiling state but that boiling still needed to stay under control. It was not the time to make any volcanic eruption. Some friends were already in tears, so we just tried to take it in a humoristic way, with some noises and jokes. Goodbyes mean a new phase, moving to a new personal adventure.

After some farewells, it was my time. Time to leave; leave the place with memories, full of humans' stories. What will you take with you down the hill; a question we reflected upon during one of the sessions. Now, it was time to go back down the hill, leave that bubble of peace, harmony and mystery. If I had never attended that program, I would have never got the opportunity to know that such a place exists.

What am I taking with me down the hill? While going down, I was trying to detach myself slowly. This is the problem of attachment! If it takes control of you, if you make it control your life, then there will be a series of pain, suffering and deceptions. I realized that nothing is permanent; giving the control of your life to a certain fact, or person is not healthy at all.

"According to Buddhist psychology, most of our troubles stem from attachment to things that we mistakenly see as permanent." Dalai Lama. What are the things you take for granted? What are you holding to strongly? What are you attached to? How can you work on being less attached?

It is important to celebrate any relation. Enjoy each moment with people we cherish, wanting the best for them. At the same time, it is important to be detached. Do not try to let your attachment, lead you to a desire for control or over protection. It is just like being a parent. Sooner or later, your kid will become an adult, he or she may have to travel for studies, work or even to create his or her own smaller family. If you love him/her, you need to equip him/her to get ready for that. Equip your child to be independent, to be analytical. Let him/her be responsible for his/her decision, taking decisions on his/her behalf will not be useful at all. Will you stay for him/her forever? Will he/she stay with you forever? Who will assist in the Farwell? Who will leave that life first? Can you have any certitude?

Our fear of losing the people we love, seeing them struggling or falling is a big pain. Sometimes such fear leads us to prepare them to be unprepared to face life circumstances. In the long run, guess what, it becomes hard for others and us as well. This situation of fear and attachment may lead to the destruction of the relation.

As I was leaving, so many events of the program were surfacing in my mind. I recalled the day when we were back from an outing with one of our trainers and we started discussing about relations and humans. Most of us were in the same train, the only difference was that we were going up the hill together, and now I was going down on my own. While observing the Swiss mountain, an analogy made its way into my mind; humans and human relations are just like these mountains. They are so close to one another, yet too far. Mountains as well, they are too close to each other, yet their peaks are so distant.

As shared by our coach, "We may have the same territory, but having different maps". We do experience the same emotions, we have the same body mechanism, yet we behave differently. There are so many factors to take into consideration, mood, belief system, values, experiences, cultures... That is why it is important to let each one experience life according to their own personal map, and not imposing our own.

We may partner together, but I will never be the leader of your life. I will be just walking beside you. At some point we will be at the peak, we may hardly find common ground and sometime later, we go back down the hill where both the mountain bottoms meet. This is the point where we can find out what connects us and start building on it. Being at the peak, being different, or seeing things differently, is not what matters. What matters is not arguing over what we see is right and what others see is wrong, forgetting that we are at two different peaks.

The problem is that we tend to focus on the who and not the what! Who is right, rather than what is right.

Then, I looked out of the train window and saw the palace towers, I was feeling so grateful for that experience, it may be the last time I was seeing it! Or, will see it again another time while going up the hill, who knows? In my handbag, an envelope was getting impatient to be read. A mystery envelope. A week in advance, envelopes had been hanged on a rope in our training room, at Salon Du Lac, each envelope with one of our names. We were requested to write down any quote, memory, compliment, positive thought, and an unforgettable moment, write the name of the envelope owner and leave there. We were asked to read the content of that envelope once we reach our home or on the way back home but not during our program. I respected it, did not read even a single word of what had been written until I boarded my second train to France. I was going back there to meet my relatives, check my expected future university and look for a studio apartment to move in the coming September.

The moment I tried to open the envelope, a passenger sat nearby and we started conversing. Normal introductions as usual, name, occupation, where will be your final destination... After some time, he decided to go and get some coffee. I thought that it was the best opportunity to finally discover my envelope mystery. So I opened it, there were many pieces of papers. Papers in different colors and shapes, just like our intern's group. Papers were different, yet the envelope was the common ground.

Our common ground was the time we passed together in the Caux Palace, discovering more about IofC and more importantly, going deeper into our purpose and self. We now had memories in common. On the bigger picture, that envelope is our world. We are all living on the earth, having it as common ground, yet being from a different part, culture, religion... What adds beauty to life is all that diversity. Let us say there are just apples as fruits, will we enjoy eating just apples daily? Let us remember the previous spring, its beauty and harmony, despite the fact that some of us may have a pollen allergy, its beauty is in all the mixed colors, flowers from different types. How will life look like if there are no colors, if all is grey? That is life's mystery of diversity, the beauty of diversity!

As I started reading the papers, suddenly a thick film of tears formed in my eyes. And yes again emotions, this time letting the volcanic eruption happen that was much needed. Mostly, I knew maybe that it would happen as I had preferred to read them when I would be alone. Just because did not want to be asked are you ok! Do you need any support? I wanted to channelize those emotions, like a river, I wanted to let them go with the stream. Some laughs, some great memories, I read all that was written. Then I closed the envelope, wiped the tears and decided to sleep as I still had hours of journey left. After the long night of writing, and several farewells, I needed to rest a little bit.

Tears, stress, laugh, anger, pain, suffering, love, like, happiness, all these are emotions and we do feel them as we all are humans. Sometimes we do divide them into negative and positive emotions. But what do you think? Should we divide them this way? Is it about emotions or about how do we embrace and react to them? We can have an excess of excitement, that may lead us to harm, as we can feel pain to overcome it, build on it and create success. On the other hand, this same excitement may lead us to more enthusiasm and achievement, as the pain may lead to depression.

Here, let me share an anonymous quote "Never reply when you are angry. Never make a promise when you are happy. Never make a decision when you are sad." So is it really about emotions? Or is it about reactions? If emotions exist, it is for a reason, imagine life without emotions, how will it look like? Will it be possible to experience happiness if there is no sadness? Will it be possible to know what does love means if there is no hate? Will it be possible to define peace without knowing what conflict means? Will it be possible to feel in harmony if you never passed through stress? What about agitation and calm?... In life, we need all this diversity. Just like day and night. Just like, we need to sleep and be awake.

What is negative or positive is not by essence, it is by reaction. Sleeping, for example, is needed, and primordial, but what about oversleeping? Then it becomes negative. So only our behaviors and attitude toward emotions make the result either positive or negative. This is why it is important to embrace our emotions, understand them and be aware that others as well do have the same system of emotions. There are several ways to make the output as positive as possible. Some may go for prayers, others for meditation, yoga, sport, running, walking, writing; the list is so long.

However, remember we do not have the same map so what works for one may not work for another. You are the only one responsible to find out how it will work for you. Having that said, it is not only about emotions but many more aspects of life. You are the only expert in your life. Others may support you, but they will never be your life's experts.

As I reached France, it was time to go back and pass some time with my relatives. Within myself, I was more into reflection mode but it was the time to live that moment of family time and enjoy my time in Paris. A good learning, just at any time, try your best to live the moment. "The secret of health for both mind and body is not to mourn for the past, worry about the future, or anticipate troubles, but to live in the present moment wisely and earnestly", Buddha.

CHAPTER EIGHT

Back to Real Life

My time in France was over. Some family shopping, visits, walks and memories to be remembered. I had visited the university, and found a studio apartment. Everything was just working perfectly, everything in my external circle, but not really the same feeling within myself. I do remember, back in Caux, when I was asked what are your upcoming plans, I replied briefly, "I will be starting a Master's Degree in the coming September." One day a new good friend asked me about my future plans. We were just two of us discussing, and I shared that there was a 90% chance that I would be enrolling for a master's degree, yet 10% chance was that I was not sure.

Within me, there was no real enthusiasm for doing it anymore. A voice was saying deep within me; it is not what you really want.

So, I was back from Caux and France to Lebanon, welcome back to life's reality. It was kind of an electrical choke, as if you are taking someone from a sauna room at high temperature, then you ask him/her to run straight to the lowest room temperature and jump into a pool full of ice cubes. Completely two different worlds, on one hand, it was a world of respect, discussion, dialogue, compassion, listening, diversity, vision, absolute values, sharing and empathy. And on the other hand, a world of power, corruption, debate, one vision centered, less chance of real communication, suffocated morals as now considered for the weak.

In our daily life, it is becoming the law of the jungle, the law of power. I do believe that all of us have felt that difference! When I discussed with some CPLP friends, even they shared the same experience. Yet, I was full of energy, enthusiasm and will to work on the change, knowing that local communities in Lebanon need to take massive steps. I started looking for social local and international movements, to be more active.

Then I get engaged in two more organizations, adding to IofC. It was a need to find out how to use this energy before it is lost. It was not that easy to find the movement I could feel connected to. I started attending meetings, and some events. After a certain meeting, while dropping one of the new colleagues to his home, we just discussed to get to know each other better. When I shared that I was alternatively working as a volunteer with IofC and also planning to get involved with another team, he insisted, "You need to focus may be on one. You should choose your priority, or it will be hard for you to contribute fully the way you want to all 3 of them."

As days and weeks passed, I found that he was right! I started feeling pressurized, low energy and unsatisfied. I remembered a local saying "You cannot carry several watermelons in your hands at the same time, or you will drop all of them, and they will break." So I decided to take the time to find out where was my priority? What was my calling? I started narrowing my commitments, the first choice was easy due to distance. The second one was harder but not really a big deal, just because what I did find within IofC I did not find it elsewhere. What are you working on currently? What are your priorities? How to create a balance between them?

The final decision was to continue with IofC. For the first few months, I was not that active, they did invite me to take part in the yearly retreat organized by the local team, but I did not attend. At that moment, it was just around a month or two after the internship experience. I was not in a mood to get exposed to others and to make new relations. I was more inclined to the need for personal space, space to take in all that had happened, reflect and digest. One of the learnings of the program was knowing yourself. Know to take care of yourself or you will not be able to take care of people around you, take care of the world. You cannot offer what you lack. During that time, I was not able to offer any kind of peace knowing within that it was not harmony.

You are the only master of your life. You may receive guidance, holly guidance, but for that, you need first to know yourself well. If at any time I am feeling pressured, lost or anxious, my surrounding will not be able to help me unless I become aware of my current situation. "I am the master of my fate: I am the captain of my soul." William Ernest Henley.

I knew that giving the lead to the outer world will just make me lose fully my compass to be able to change the world, I needed to first understand what was going on in my inner world, and work on bringing peace there. I was aware that it was not an easy task, a lifelong process, continuous process, daily input, daily challenges and temptations, until passing away, the process will be still ongoing. That was the month full of reflections, and what was entirely taking my focus was the master program. In fact even if all was planned, within me there were that small voice saying to not go for it. I had to take a final decision before the end of the month. If it was a yes, I would have to go back to Gabon, to apply for my student visa from there.

It was not easy to handle. There was a conflict between my aspirations and what the society had planned for me. It was quite exhausting because it has to be that way and not because you wanted it to be like that. What else should I dream of or wanted to plan for? From where I come, it is a privilege to go to any country in Europe. First high academic curriculum, and second who knows maybe after your degree you may work there. Europe a well-developed Union, with a strong economy and good organization. Some may say that at least human rights there are fully respected.

When I applied and got accepted, I was one of those thinking that way. It was about leaving challenges behind, expecting that it will be a perfect life there. Forgetting an important fact that challenges will arise anywhere, and my role will be to overcome them. Each time I got new learnings, achievements and successes. According to Joshua J. Marine "Challenges are what make life interesting and overcoming them is what makes life meaningful."

Let's go to our memories, how do we feel when everything is just perfect? Then how do we feel after an achievement? How it looks like overcoming a certain challenge? In life, there is always a good sequence of things happening with each one of us.

On a night, I was sitting with my brother and his friend. We started discussing about my travel, my reasons... We ended our discussion with my friend's brother saying "If you are going because you want to go is one thing, but if you are going just because there are no other opportunities, then it's a different story." Then we started discussing about other things.

However, afterward, I got into a self-reflection mode. What is my purpose? Why am I going there? Am I really satisfied? At that time, I was still looking for a job, it was not easy to find any. Maybe that was what was pushing me to go. Maybe it was just because according to the society's concept, you need to go for a master after your bachelor's degree. What about the program I will be enrolled in? Is it really what I want? All those questions were asked on daily basis; they were just like a train encircling in my mind on high speed.

With time, I got clarity, and felt happier; still was thinking of how to communicate the final decision to my family? A transfer for my accommodation was done, to confirm that I will be using the location starting from September. Everything was just as planned. Then on a day, I received an email informing that as I did not make a payment transfer, the studio apartment would be rented to a new lodger. I took it as the best time to make my final decision. I requested to check the transaction history and found what was written in the email was correct. Something went wrong while making the transfer, so it had not been sent. One of my family members said that it was ok, I could call the owner, find another apartment, or even stay in a hostel for the initial period while looking for a final place to stay in.

So I replied to the email, stating that the apartment was not needed anymore, as I would not be going in the coming year. I thought that maybe the apartment issue was just a sign to not go. As usual, some of my family members were happy to hear that decision, and others just wondered what was happening. Who can lose such an opportunity? You are crazy! It will be hard to do anything and expecting everyone to support your decision in the end.

At that moment, I was not in a mood to explain my decision, especially knowing that the home was divided with two completely different opinions. So days before my travel back to Gabon, I decided to cancel my ticket, and from that moment I just felt better, calmer and more at peace with myself, despite the chaos around. Yes, it was still possible to change things. Things can maybe change but not my decision. In each decision, it is important to consider the pros and cons especially when it is about your personal life or connected to your own purpose.

You must consider what is the reason behind each decision? Each action? How will it support you in reaching your purpose? Any decision that may look great to you but not matching with your life purpose will mostly end up causing more harm than good. It will make you feel happy at the beginning as any new experience, then you will find yourself buried under continuous stress.

Therefore, it is always good to take time to reflect on important decisions in life. Give it enough time, but at the same time, assign a deadline to yourself, to be able to evaluate your progress in each situation. The more it is in an open frame, the more we may take it easy, or tend to overload ourselves. The more time will pass with that overload, the harder it will be for us to bear its weight.

An important aspect is always to think about our real motive behind each step. Some friends do ask me until now, do you regret that decision? And my reply is, "What will regret bring to my life? How will it support my purpose?" In life, regrets may show up many times, what is important is to transform them into learnings. Also, it is important to know that living the past again is not possible, instead focus on what outputs can you take from the past. A certain decision taken, a project cancelled, it will not be the end of life. What other doors do you see open, and if none, which door can you open? Bob Marley once said, "When one door is closed, don't you know, another is open." So, let's try to focus on the open doors while learning from each closed one. What are the learnings of your previous experiences? How did you find out a new open door, or doors to open repeatedly? What is supporting you to keep on going?

CHAPTER NINE

Break Year

A year of preparation

A year before the program, I was waiting for that moment, getting graduated, starting a new job, started building a career path. Plans were set, enthusiasm high, yet the reality was not expected that way. Finding a training or job in Lebanon was not that easy. After a discussion, the decision was to go back to Gabon; my second homeland and try my chance there. It was an easy move, my relatives were still there, a welcoming atmosphere.

In the beginning it was normal, a long process of looking for a job. I said to myself "it needs time". I was applying without getting any reply. While looking for internships and jobs, I found myself enjoying my personal time. It was the time to run, walk and reflect. The natural beauty of the country was supporting me in that. We were living on the coastal side. Each walk was a source of new energy, a source of deeper connection. The sound of the waves, wind dance, leading the steps of coconut trees leaves, blue sky with a shiny sun, just a bubble of hope. A habit had been created for a few months. I had developed a daily ritual, waking up before the sunrise and at the end of the day connecting to sunset. Each new day, it was a new masterpiece drawn in the sky. It was not possible to get enough of those beauties, that harmony.

So many questioning and reflections started to surface at that point. Why each day there is a new harmonious sunrise? Why each day ends with the sunset? Night! Day! Connection! Complementarity! Biodiversity! Diversity! Life! Purpose! I cannot remember all that was turning on in my small mind. One of the reflections was to connect each sunrise with a new hope, a hope for a better life, a better future. There is always a new dawn; after each night a new day will rise.

At some point, life may not be that easy, we may feel like living in complete obscurity, yet believe that each darken tunnel has an ending, an enlightened exit or entry. That's what brings the sunset. Time to go to obscurity, as to say that those challenging periods are needed to bring the best out of them, the best deep in us. I do think that this quote from an unknown author is deeply rooted to the Holy Bible "God sometimes takes us into troubled water not to drown us but to cleanse us.". Just like olive oil, this component was important in several cultures before our time and even until now. We do enjoy having olive oil in many of our plates, soaps, creams...How easy it is to make olive oil? Not easy at all! Here you go with the different steps to pass by: 1) crush olives into a paste 2) mix the paste with hot water 3) grind it, until seeing beads of oil on the surface 4) vigorously stir paste until larger beads of oil are formed 5) drain 6) siphon the oil... Out life is just like the olive and olive oil, to get the essence of our deep humanity, spirituality and productivity, we need to pass through all those steps. We need to stay strong during the first 4 steps, overcome the challenges and at the surface from deep within will then float our essence. Yet it will not be enough, while draining and siphoning, we may decide either to focus on water and paste, or to take care of the found olive oil, store it and know how to use it. Knowing that the remaining paste can be used as well, it highlights the point or learning from each situation.

Like after any sunset, the night will start, just to give time to rest, and reflect, maybe to ask yourself what needs to be improved, changed, corrected to create a better you with the coming sunrise. Always keep in mind, whatever happens, will pass and a new day will shine. This new day may be a blessing, having a new opportunity for extra time on our earth. As well it can be a new day, just in another dimension. In any case, it will be our duty to create our own olive oil from our life. Life will not be easy; we just need to work on being stronger. Adding to contemplation and walking soon started a hobby of long runs.

It was becoming my habit, of always giving more and challenging the body and the mind. The more I was giving energy, the more I was feeling satisfied. Meanwhile, I was taking time to read and research more. I was more interested in psychology, philosophy, religion, and world situation. It was great soaking in all that self-time, just peacefully discovering more about my interest, life, and taking time to question myself.

Then my first internship started, it was not that much demanding. It was more about office work: archives, organize documents, payroll and simple duties. Three months later, at the end of this first internship started a completely different experience. I got another three months of internship in one of the biggest business groups. My role there was polyvalent, every three weeks I was alternating and shifting to a new department. In the beginning it was exciting, and in the last month it turned to be more reflective. Reflecting on what I was doing, is it aligned with my purpose? Is life really about having a job, a salary, some profits? What am I adding to life? To the Society? Any added contribution offered? I found out that it was 'no' as an answer.

A relevant learning was the interdependence factor. I had worked in different departments with strengthened actions and learned the importance of connection. If any action at any department was delayed, all the others were affected as well. That is not only in the case of business, it is also in the case of our life. Each action may take us nearer to our goal, or repulse us from it. Each of our actions will have an effect on us, and as well it will affect our surroundings, others humans, animals and nature. Everything in life is a cycle.

This period was mostly preparing me for what I would be discovering at Caux. It was making me get used to self-reflection. After my internship, it was another kind of reflection. It was a reflection on what do I really wanted?

What kind of contribution I wanted to offer? What are my values? My beliefs? Who am I really deep within me? Since then I decided to make a shift from business opportunities to social contributions, so I started applying to social job opportunities more than focusing on a stable business career. It was at that time when I found that some of my values were shaking. What was happening? Why am I acting that way? Am I satisfied? It was just the "I want to be like others" wish. I wanted to be like anyone else in the society. I wanted to feel normal. Saying normal is just a copy of the shaped same human product. Like any product, we humans can become just a brand with a specific packaging that is reproduced. Here questioning myself was important! Why did I walk against my values? Did I hurt any other human's dignity? How to get back to those -golden-self values? Maybe I still do not have some answers. Maybe at some point, it was done unconsciously. Some completely in a conscious state.

I remember, the ones I was not connected to, I would write small sorry letters and apologies. It is not an easy task to put your pride aside, take away your higher Ego and apologize. A tool that supported me was the virtual platform, as it was easier for me to write and send a message or email instead of calling or meeting to share my thoughts. And when it was connected to the self, it was important to dig deep within, find out the real motive to check if it aligns with my values, and if not, working on stepping back to the path I wanted to be on. That does not mean that it was the ultimate self-purification. That does not mean that I am now a perfect man, we are all humans. There are always temptations, reactions, circumstances, emotions. So, I was trying to be more aware of the fact that each one of them is a great beginning. It will be easy to go back for a mistake and even easier when we are not aware that it is a mistake.

As shared previously everything in life is continuous and a cycle. That self-reflection, self-correction, will always be my companion, there will always be ways of more purification. It was at that time when my quest for real self-balance started. Desires and needs, what is the difference? How to find an equilibrium? What relation exists between desires, needs, brain and mind? What is the difference between animals and humans? Animals are the creatures living by instincts, their level of desire may be high, they may not differentiate between their desire and needs. Humans, on the other hand, with the added piece called mind , are given the opportunity to differentiate between the two. The more we are driven by our desires, the less we are satisfied, the more we want.

Fire normally gives light, it supports to cook and to keep warm. What will happen if the fire grows bigger, and out of the circle of equilibrium. The more it becomes bigger, the more it can affect the surrounding. The more it spans, the harder it will be to control it. During this year and every year, there are myriad instances of huge fires. The destruction is just huge; in some cases, it takes days to extinguish it fully. Nature, animals, lands, properties, human victims, there is a huge loss, the effect prevails even after a few months. After the fire is controlled, what is left behind is ashes, corpses and debris. You may not see it the same way; you may have other analogies, but let me link it to desires. When they take control of us, they may affect the outer world first, but at the same time, they affect our body, mind and soul. It is like sugar, the more our body will take, the more will be craving to get more. And again if the effects do not show up directly, they will appear with time. Here it is the beginning of the questioning. How to equilibrate desires and needs? What is the connection that exists between Mind, Body and Spirit? Will it be possible to find it? Moreover, how to live that equilibrium and connection?

CHAPTER TEN

Back to Caux

2015 was over, before welcoming 2016, the application for the Caux forum 2016 had been rolled out. I was wishing to take part in the forum, but that year was not an easy year. I was back in Lebanon, contributing to the family business and still looking for a job. Even if during the Caux forum the family business is generally close, but it was not possible for me to make it. I was not in a position to offer myself a ticket to be able to fly there. Within myself, I was feeling that connection to the place, that wish to be there again but I knew that I needed to stay realistic and accept the fact that it will not be possible for this year. In my mind, it was not this year, but if God sees that it will be a good step to pass through again, it will happen in the coming years. From my first internship different, great and precious relations had been built. Some of those friends, we are still connected now, whereas I had lost contact with others due to personal responsibilities. Even if I was not in touch, still, out of nowhere, I would feel that connection, thoughts just popped into my mind and I would send prayers to all.

While writing, I am reminded of the day when we had a water battle game. The atmosphere was full of joy, energy and enthusiasm. When the game was over, I found out that I had lost my locket during the game. I felt sad about it and decided to start looking for it. It was not about the locket but more about the ring in it, as it was a gift from my grandmother. A gift that is precious for me. Then I started asking if anyone had seen it. I was shocked to see that even they started looking for it with me. We were playing outside, in a completely open place, so it was not that easy to find it. Sunset had started, at that moment, I decided to stop looking for it as there was no ample light. And I said to myself, if it is meant to be found, it will be. I started asking friends to stop looking for it, it was time for a real shower. Suddenly, a friend came, saying he had get it, it was near to the water tape. I am still grateful for it, at that moment I just felt in harmony like the beauty of the sunset.

You never know when and where will be the next opportunity that may let you feel at peace and in harmony. It was unexpected, despite the fact that it was not in the plan but I was able to make it for the Forum in 2016. I received a call from a dear friend, asking me if would you like to be back for the coming forum? And then I shared about my situation, so she said, "Let me check about it and I will come back to you." At that moment it was still possible to apply as a volunteer to be back. That means that you will be serving while your accommodation and food will be taken care of, but still, you needed to pay for your travel. I was not having any problem with going as a volunteer, being back there, in that multicultural space will be again an added learning experience, but paying for the ticket was not possible for me.

A couple of days later, she contacted me back saying, "If you really want to be back, and are motivated about it, do not worry about your ticket, we will take care of it." It was just a personal miracle happening. A miracle is not just something super-ordinary, it may also be an ordinary thing happening unexpectedly. Sometimes wish and will are what are needed from our side, all the rest is being worked out, and taken care of from a higher power. In such situations, faith and trust are needed.

I learned more about the importance of relationship, unconditional relationship and goodwill. It is like the law of attraction, what you believe in, you will attract it. I got the chance to be back to the Caux forum in 2016, 2017, 2019 and I was planning to be there again for 2020 as part of the hospitality team but you know well that the entire world's plans for 2020 had been changed.

Each year, when I was back, it was a new learning. The first year I was just an intern so I did just live the beauty of the programs. While during the following years, I was more aware of the team's responsibilities to create that atmosphere of beauty. Preparations start a year in advance, content, programs, invitations, panellist, teams, participants, selections, updates, changes, adaptations. None of the years have happened without any change, it was a constant seeking to always creating the best experience for all. It was not an easy task and it is still not easy as there are always changes to make, always looking for a better version than the previous year. At some point, it was challenging, at others, it was easy going, the most important task was to work as a team.

Within Initiatives of change, it was great to experience how hard can be that change. It will not happen overnight; it is a long process. That is maybe the reason behind each year trying to make the best to adapt to the external factors while working on making an internal shift for a better forum.

If I have to rate my different experiences, the most challenging one was in 2017, due to the fact that many changes were happening at the same time, the transition was not easy, yet we were able to survive, experience and learn from the forum. Chapeau bas for a team that was always supportive. Without great team support, it would have been just not possible to make it. From those several experiences, some major learnings are whatever you are doing important is to create a strong team, the change will never be easy, each day is a new opportunity to work on yourself, just like the forum, there will always be changes to be made on a personal level. It is easier to work on yourself than on people around you.

Let's start with the importance of the team, look at the bird's migration movement. They fly together in a way that you cannot be aware of the challenges they are facing while flocking. They support each other's move. Each move and position is directed to make others around at ease.

Being in the hospitality team made me realize the importance of always doing the duty fully, in that way, it will be easier for the next team in charge to take over. Always leave your workplace as you would like to come and find it. Try always to simplify the life of the ones in charge after you. It is not only about hospitality, and work, it becomes a life rule as well. How will you feel when starting a new job, with a ready desk welcoming you? Organized tools ready for you to be used? Organized files? Back home how will you feel when you find the home welcoming you in order? How will you feel having to do an already done duty, because it has been disorganized? How will you feel going to the public garden and finding it clean, ready to let you enjoy your time? As it becomes a golden rule, to make it easier for the person taking over, it is the same in the case of life we are living! What kind of life would you want the coming generation to take over from you? While talking about heritage, how are your actions shaping that world heritage?

In that forum, something that was creating that good team atmosphere and trust was our family time. As a practice, each department, each team, was having a family time on a weekly basis. It was the time to come together and just have fun; relish snacks, story sharing, personal experiences, activities and games. That was creating stronger bonds even if we were aware that our teamwork will just be for a month or two. Discovering more of our different stories was supporting our human relationship rather than just teamwork group.

What about change? Any change from a small habit to a bigger project, will not be easy. It is mostly for that, at least 40 days are needed to be able to change an old habit and to replace it with another. Any change will demand resistance and it will need persistence, resilience, flexibility and maybe some logic. Third, like anything in life, each one of us is in continuous changing phases. From baby to kid, then teenager, youth, adult, elder... Change is not only on at the biological level, but it is as well on mental, emotional and spiritual dimension.

Each new day brings to us new experiences, experiences that support our growth on all the levels and can even make a complete shift, leading to a new realization. A realization that may lead to a personal change. There are always personal discoveries that we do about ourselves. For that, you can use the Johari Windows activity, repeat it after 3 months and then again do it to see that results and finding may be changing. Basically, the Johari Windows activity does play on four aspects, Open area, Hidden area, Blind Area and Unknown area. Finally, it is easier to work on self-reactions than putting all the expectations on the surroundings. Why? Because there may be too many aspects that you may be unaware of about the others, their situations, the mood they are in. It is already a hard task to work on self-reactions and responses but it is practically impossible to work on or control other's reactions.

Always keep in mind that as you are in a complete daily transformation and transition mode, others are as well.

On a day, the manager shared with our team, "You are working in hospitality industry, it is a hard work, and just keep in mind that any feedback you receive, do not take it personally." That became another golden rule for me. Not only about not taking feedback personally but more into knowing how to create a self-strong protective shield. Feedbacks can be received daily, will you let them affect your stability? Will you let them affect your harmony? Will you let them affect your wellbeing? How can you work on creating your self-protective shield? What can make your shield strong enough and resistant to the outer obstacles? Knowing that you are the only one aware of it fully, aware of its importance, you are the only one who can create it.

CHAPTER ELEVEN

University Experience

High school was achieved; it was the time for a normal transition that any student looks for. It was a normal one, yet a difficult step to be clear of. For several years, I was having an objective to pursue in the business domain. Yet the questions were where? How? Which University? I was aware of the family situation, when it comes to the economic level, the situation was not that simple. For that, I did not want to be pushy, and even I was not having the motivation to look for programs. I did start the academic year on the midway, starting in the second semester. It was hard for me to apply at the Public local university back in Lebanon, the reason was my difficulties with Arabic. In fact, what supported me to keep speaking Arabic was the practice at home but I have never been enrolled in Arabic classes.

At that point, I was able to express myself and understand verbal communication, but it was hard for me to write and it was taking too much time for me to read. I did not take the Arabic course during my earlier academic phase, yet I was grateful to be able to communicate at least. I did start with an accounting major then a year later, I decided to change major.

I decided to go more into relation than numbers, so I ended up doing international business management. During my second year, I decided to check again in the public local university if I can, by chance, find majors delivered in

French or English related to philosophy or psychology that I could get enrolled in as a second major. The campus I checked with, which was the nearest to my place, the answer was negative. So the idea of doing double major get erased quickly.

Starting a career in major is a step that every student may be impatient to jump in, yet a decisive one. So many times, we take it just because we have to, we should, the society imposes it on us, or we do not have any other option. I never had any career guidance and I do believe that it is the same case for so many of us previously and maybe even until now. Career guidance does not mean university promotions, rather sharing with students about options they may have, new opening majors, the situation of the market and so on. Actually, because of this, we do tend to reach a point of dissatisfaction with what we are doing, then we decide to change the career path. Some may change it at the earlier stage while still studying in 2nd or 3rd year while others may do it after a working experience.

Here, to avoid such a situation, it is important to take time reflecting on what you want. Your real purpose in life? What do you enjoy doing? These are important because your career will be taking a huge part of your future life. And if you are not able to find satisfaction within your career, your life will just be a full package of stress and dissatisfaction. That's what took me from business, to social work, then to the training field to end up now in the coaching path. Who knows some new updates, and new skills may need new learnings as well. "Find out what you like doing best, and get someone to pay you for doing it."-Katharine Whitehorn. Just walk through your passion, earnings will come through it. If our focus is just on earning, we are on the way to losing passion. What will you be left with after losing our passion?

During my university period, I was getting more and more introverted. It is maybe due to the cultural difference as the first reason. I had grown up in a traditional Lebanese way, yet I did live the cultural diversity at school and with my friends. My perception of things, habits, ways of expression were not fully the same. For instance, in Lebanon, it is normal when two men greet each other, they kiss the cheek, which was not the case back in Gabon. So one day, I do remember that I repulsed a friend who came to greet me in the Lebanese way. Another day, for example, I was asked about my backpack. "You are at university, you are not a kid anymore, so why do you come to university with a backpack? I tried to understand the relation between bag, university and kids but did not find any, then I did explain that using a bag is just for my self-comfort. I turned to become unsocial with a tendency to escape through my earphones and music.

The administration wanted to talk to me on another day, so they requested another student to call me. And as that student didn't know me he was asked to look for the one with a black bag, cup, long hair and earphones.

Our campus was small so it was an easy task to locate the person with that description. While trying to step out of my comfort zone, I went to one of the trips organized by the university, but then I did not enjoy it much, I found that I do not really enjoy parties, high music sound and there it was not possible to plug in the earphone. It was not about being good or bad, it was just about preferences, each one may find joy in different things. One may find joy with parties, another with a cup of coffee or another one will be better while hiking, and some enjoy reading. It was just about knowing the real self, to find out the source of joy. "Wanting to be someone else is a waste of the person you are."-Kurt Cobain. What do give you real satisfactions and joy? How do you like to spend your free time?

Another aspect that had affected me was the fact of political division. Unfortunately, I discovered that Lebanon is divided into colors. I did grow up far from all that, I was aware of it, but I did not know how deeply it is rooted. At some point, I started following the dance, but quickly decided that I cannot follow blindly, we are all humans and it is our right to express our disagreement even when it comes to people we may consider as leaders.

Unfortunately, that was not really accepted; if you disagree, it means that you are against, it is either white or black and it was forgotten that colors are in multiples, especially in a highly diverse and politically divided Lebanon. To be at peace with myself, I decided to stay neutral and even then, at some point, I was considered wrong, as you have to choose a certain party, or you are just a traitor for all. You need to be in one party, holding on to your beliefs, pull along to your direction while other parties also pull along their own side and look at Lebanon just being teared up. More pulling are being strong, the deeper the wounds, the more is the bleeding.

In a way, we did keep on pulling to lead where we are now, in 2020, Lebanon is in reanimation and needs more care than ever. Will that critical situation wake us up? Will it make us put our self-benefits and political differences apart, come together and find out how to support Lebanon? Will it be the transition to rebirth or will we keep dying? It is too easy to throw the responsibility of the current situation on others but that will not be of any support.

The first step for a rebirth is to take the responsibility, start from each one deficiency, as our current situation is just an accumulation, and each one of us has a part of the responsibility, we did all contribute to what had happened to the country. This situation is seen everywhere, in each country and even on a global level. Talking about a better future may be easy, but what about our responsibilities in creating it? Sustainable development, sustainable life, responsible consumption, peaceful earth.... Will all that happen without personal awareness? Personal commitment? Personal responsibilities? Will that happen without learning what does it mean to be a good life citizen? How will it be possible to create it, without sacrifices, change in habits and comfort?

Finally, starting my bachelor's degree, took me from a house where everything came to me at the snipe of fingers, to a place where I needed to go to things, create them. That as well may have contributed to the fact of becoming introvert at that moment. The first academic year, I had the company of my brother but then I was alone, living like any young student adapting to a new way of life. Before my academic studies, my duties were just to study without having any other big responsibility as my mom and my elder brothers were taking care of everything else. Back in that period, my life was purely based on home, school, studies, some cousins, and lately in the period some outing with friends. So the huge part of my time was between home and school, which shaped me as well to become a homebody, so outer socializing was not always my strength.

That way of living created a small safe zone, a small comfort zone for me, which increased my fear zone. That fear zone travelled with me, then with time, I had to work on reducing it by taking more responsibilities, and reshaping my personality. With time, confidence started to grow, I do remember a day when one of my instructors at university shared with me "You need to be confident, and believe in what you do." That was shared after a small presentation I had delivered.

It is easy at some point for parents to complain about children. Complaining about confidence, responsibility level, actions, behavior... but how did the Children reach the point they could complain? How has his/her personality been shaped? Personality gets shaped from an earlier age. If we want a child to be responsible and confident, we need to let him/her feel it since the beginning. Working on critical thinking, decision-making, giving responsibilities, making our kids involved in our home life. It is not that easy to be parents, I do not think that there is a perfect rule or equation, and I do believe that if a decision has been taken to become parents, that means that your life is not any more yours but theirs. Your life's objective becomes to create the best for your kids, creating the best may mean to make sacrifices, and let them experience life.

"Your children are not your children. They are the sons and daughters of Life's longing for itself. They come through you but not from you, and though they are with you, yet they belong not to you. You may give them your love, but not your thoughts. For they have their own thoughts. You may house their bodies but not their souls, for their souls dwell in the house of tomorrow, which you cannot visit, not even in your dreams. You may strive to be like them, but seek not to make them like you. For life goes not backward, nor tarries with yesterday."-Khalil Gibran.

How complex it is to be a parent! Each one wanting to do the best. Each has his own way to do the best, protection, guidance, prohibition, care, support, rewards, punishment. What do you think is the best way of parenting? How to be the best while supporting your kid to be the best, and give the best?

CHAPTER TWELVE

High School

I do not remember much of the early stage of my primary phase. It was shared between Lebanon and Gabon. It was fixed and definitive to move to Gabon when I was around 9 years old. During this time, we moved and stayed there longer. I did stay until the end of 2008 or may be beginning of 2009. My primary and secondary school has been explored in Gabon, a country that became my second home. At 9 years old, when we moved, it was in the mid of the scholastic year, I went with my mother to the director of a primary school for my inscription. There the question was "Should I get enrolled and continue the curriculum I started in Lebanon, or should I go back to the previous level?" Then after a long discussion with the director, after sharing the curriculum and books I was using, the decision was made that I will get a chance before the final decision. They decided that I will get enrolled in the same class for a month and according to the results, the final decision will be taken. It was not that easy, as I was moving from a curriculum with partial French classes to a curriculum fully in French. So yes, I was having difficulties in French, but I said to myself that I can do it.

What supported me was my ability in math and science, also teachers and friends were really supportive. With each transition, at each level, there will always be challenges to be overcome. What adults may consider as simple could be challenges for kids and youth. With each challenge, there will always be tools, support and opportunities around, but important is the will to overcome them deep within.

"If you expect life to be easy, challenges will seem difficult. If you accept that challenges may occur, life will be easier."- Rob Liano

With all the support I got, the personal will and continuous studying, my marks were reflecting my hard work, responsibility and seriousness, so the final decision was to stay in the same class and not to go a level back. A great first success!

After the primary school was over, it was time to pass the public exam and get ready for secondary school. At that time, a test had to be passed to be able to get accepted in secondary schools. Nowadays some countries still have that test whereas others do not have it anymore. I did apply and passed it successfully. In the form we filled, we selected 3 public secondary schools in the order of priority. My first priority was in Lycée d'Application Nelson Mandela (LANM). At that time, this secondary school was considered one of the best in in terms of education. I got accepted to be a part of LANM, yet the question was, 'will I start my college cycle there, or should I find another school?' It was a debate at home! Fear of cultural difference and protective parental emotions started to play. Then the final decision was to try, and check if I will be able to adapt or not.

The first few days were not that easy, I still remember my first day, I got down from the car, I was having stomach pain, I looked to the portal, took a deep breath and started my walk to get to my class. That was a five-minute walk, during my walk in the court my name was “the white”. For a few days, I marched to my class without turning right or left, I think I was the first student with completely different origins. Now that I am thinking about it, I was the minority, I was a minority but not for long. I am reminded of my little niece’s words that made us laugh, “When we were coming to pick you up, it was easy to find you, we just had to look for the little white dot coming down.”

I made some friends in my classroom, then quickly I had friends from different classes, different levels. My name changed then from “the white” to “Hamza”. I became a part of the whole campus, but what does it mean to be part of a minority? To be different? Knowing that in the history many people felt discriminated? They felt a part of the minority, they felt the push of power on them. They felt that they could not voice their thoughts, feelings as they are less important than others. It is still the case in several places in our current world, and even maybe everywhere. We have that tendency of superiority feeling, a feeling of being better than others. I had the opportunity to travel to different countries and it was possible to feel this thick line. This line exists because the humans are treated differently according to the origins. Throughout history, deep wounds had been created due to that difference, to a certain kind of oppression. In my early college time, I did not feel anything related to that, as I had good relations with everyone. All was going well until having some incidences that happened when I was in BAC I.

The first one was the day after my afternoon class. I was going down with a friend to go home. At that time, I had started taking a taxi, public transportation. As we lived nearby we went back home together when finishing our assignments at the same time. While I and my friend were going down the court, two of my colleagues were coming up, one of them had consumed alcohol, and he was not in his conscious. He started shouting, "All is your fault, you have come to destroy our country, it is all about the white." At that moment my friend just calmed me down and requested me not to reply.

After that incident, I was in pain within. How deeply our wounds can be stored? How easy is it to feel and recognize a wounded friend, human? How can alcohol affect us? How alcohol can take us back deep into our wounds, while making them drive our actions? On another day, I was with the same friend, taking a taxi back home, and then a drunk stranger just started shouting, "It is your fault, you had stolen my house and you had stolen even my wife." While we were taking the taxi, he ran and closed the taxi door on my leg. Here again, I felt hurt for no reason, hurt for what I hadn't done. Two or three similar circumstances happened, always making me feel worse. One other circumstance that made me feel bad, was when a new student, asked me, "Why are you in a public school? Why aren't you in a private high school?" At that time, I took it as an offense as it was a way of saying that my place is not there . All those happenings made me feel uncomfortable within and I started to neglect my studies. My degrees started to plunge, but I did not share all those incidents with anyone, especially not with my family. I was repeating to myself always that all would be all right, having great supportive friends was always a release; I was neglecting the fact that each incidence was creating a deeper wound. Friends with whom I never had troubles, with whom until now and even after being in different countries for more than 10 years, we still have close relations. Even recently, I got a connection on social media and it was one of my high school friends; what a pleasure it was to be connected and share some updates and remember some memories. All those great friends, moment we cherished together, all that was what made me realize that it is not possible to generalize, it is not about all but each one's actions . And what about those actions that may hurt? What is their source deep within? Why is the person behaving that way? How our wounds are affecting our life? And how at many time we get wounded for things we did not do? Sometimes it is easy to understand and at times, not really. When it is an unshared personal wound, it will be hard to understand, but when it is more of a historical, political, social, wound it is easier to find out the reason. What about all those wounds, how to heal them? Who can heal them? Should they keep on being transferred from generation to another?

As I said earlier, my grades were falling, at the end of the year; my annual average was around nine , so under 10 means under average as the full mark was 20. Therefore, the decision was that I had to redouble. At that time, with the previous experience, reduplicating was not a good situation, it would not be supporting my psychological spirit. So then to not redouble, I decided to change from Science class to Economics and to change my high school to a small private high school near my home, 7 minutes far by walk. It was easy to get enrolled in that school without reduplicating, as by chance, the director was the same as that of my primary school and he knew that I am a hard worker. So I got enrolled and completed my Baccalauréat ES (Economic).

That year, changes were happening on a personal level as well. I was erasing so many personal values or putting them aside to be like the society, like others, trying to be a macho. Few times cheating, lying, using bad words, bad jokes, a try to smoke or to taste the alcohol but luckily I did not find joy or taste in that. And even getting into a relationship just to have a Partenaire . As being 16, 17, or 18 without being in a relationship was considered abnormal. The last one is one aspect of my life that I feel sorry for, why? Because this selfish action of conformity had mostly created wounds for others, even if apologies were asked but at that time, a huge hurt might have been felt. At that time, I was fully selfish and with a lack of values, with a lack of identity, a lack of purpose and life's meaning. At least now when I recall it, I feel that about the Hamza of that moment. That Society that I was trying to conform to was not just the different culture, I found in my early secondary school, that society now that I am thinking of it, is the society that can be found everywhere, in each country, in each place. It will be always a choice to make, either to have high standards, ethics and values or just follow our desires and instinct. It is to follow our consciousness or to be a selfish devil.

It is not an easy decision, all of us pass through it mostly when we are young and that battle continues all over our life. It needs perseverance, strengths and a good will to not fall into the trap. "Right is right, even if everyone is against it, and wrong is wrong, even if everyone is for it."- William Penn.

All that made me realize how important is to feel supported, and in good relation deep within. It made me realise that our world and each person is living a personal story, personal struggle while being on a healing process that may take a lifetime. It made me realise that if I had some hard experiences that does not erase the entire good one I had. If a person hurt me that does not mean at all that all the persons from the same group of people should be holded accountable for the action. It is not healthy to judge and generalize an entire group of person based on some experiences, as just as the fingers in our hands are different, people from same family, region or group are different. Not all hold on the same wounds and not all are passing through the same healing process. Gabon is my second country and will always be, just like in Lebanon and all others country history had wounded human deeply. The healing process will need time, compassion and a lot of empathy.

CHAPTER THIRTEEN

Initiatives of Change and Reflection Time

I had mentioned earlier as well about the Initiatives of Change (IofC), previously it started with the Oxford group, earlier it was called Moral rearmament and finally now known as IofC. It had started with Frank Buchman affirming, "A divine purpose exists for the world and each one in it", he also connected faith to societal changes. For Frank Buchman, when the European nations were re-armed for war, he called for "moral and spiritual re-armament" as the way to build a "hate-free, fear-free, greed-free world". It all started from a personal experience of Frank Buchman, an experience that took him from bitterness to spiritual connection, personal reflection and finally ended with actions. After that process, he decided to write letters to express that bitterness to his previous colleagues, and since the time he wrote them down and sent them, he felt a spiritual release. A weight and burden that he was experiencing for long, without getting any scientific explanation, he found how to let it go, he found a spiritual cure. "I am not a product of my circumstances. I am a product of my decisions."-Stephen Covey.

What is the Quiet time or reflection time? It is a common practice shared by all the IofC family members. It can be individual or in a group, open or guided. It is the time when you must slow down and listen. Generally, a big number of people practice that individually, daily in the morning when the mind is still, clear and open. It can be also done during the day or even at the end of the day.

So, what do we listen to?

We listen to our consciousness, our inner voice, God speaking to us. It is also a self-scanning process; a process to reconsider our actions, to try working on a better self. What should I do better? Any correction to do? What about appreciations? Am I living according to the 4 absolute standards? PHUL; which in Hindi means flower: Purity, Honesty, Unselfishness and Love. When it is done in a group, after the time of reflection, there is an open safe space created for sharing, and when individually or when anyone is feeling challenged, a choice can be to go and share with a close fellowship member.

We do believe that sharing our vulnerabilities and challenges make us feel stronger, it makes us reflect on the way to deal with them. A guided reflection time may start with a personal story, music, song, or quote, it may also be a question or a series of questions.

How to do it in the traditional IofC way? The answer is simple, while writing down our thoughts in our notebook. You will easily find a notebook around you.

Why to write down?

First, it is a release, second, it may support in evaluating thought's progress. Many times, the same thought may rise during several instances with days of interval. It may mean that it is really affecting us and there is a need to listen deeply to find out what to do. "When man listens, God Speaks; when man obeys, God acts; when man prays, God empowers."- E. Stanley Jones.

Sharing may not only be personal support, but it may also support others challenged by a similar situation. For that reason, the human library is really important, each human is a book full of experiences. After reading a few IofC human books, I have got the opportunity to discover. I can say that they are golden books, and it is always a learning to discover new ones or even more pages of the already read human books. Don't forget that each upcoming new page depends on the current page. "The future depends on what you do today."-Mahatma Gandhi.

Service is an important part of IofC culture, hierarchy is not present between us, we are all life's servants, we are all God's servants. Serving means contributing to creating a better self, society and world. It means being ready to support each other, being complementary. That's the magic of being at the Caux Palace in Switzerland, one of the most important IofC centers. A center that has been bought by the generosity and hard work of hundreds of Swiss citizens. There you can find near to you a mayor, businessman, Forum director, farmer, lawyer, doctor and many such personalities serving Ice Cream. The hospitality team alone will be struggling especially when the house is full of 350 participants and more. Dishwashing, cleaning up and setting up the dining room, serving, each service counts and makes it a warm place to be in. "I slept and

I dreamed that life is all joy. I woke and I saw that life is all service. I served and I saw that service is joy."-Khalil Gibran.

Another big center is at Asia Plateau (AP) in India. At Caux basically, the main event is the Caux forum during summer while the AP programs happen throughout the year, several internship batches with several conferences (international, for farmers, teachers, officers, businessman...), another program delivered in both centers is the CAUX Scholar program.

What is IofC? Initiatives of Change (IofC) is a worldwide movement of people from diverse cultures and backgrounds, who are committed to the transformation of society through changes in human motives and behavior, starting with their own. It is a movement based on moral, spiritual and ethical principles. Cultural and religious differences are respected, and the beauty is when they are shared. In fact, bridges cannot be built if a safe space for sharing our differences is not created. We always tend to fear the unknown, so together, let's make it known.

IofC is a lifelong process, once you feel connected to it, you will feel the need for continuous self-progress, for a better world. With IofC each one of us is responsible, and it is only when each one takes his/her part of the responsibility that we will be able to create a better world. The first responsibility is to start within. With IofC, I have learned that I am a victim only if I decide to be a victim, as in all circumstances I can decide to be a change-maker rather than a victim. Now IofC is present in more than 60 countries around the world, few centers, some emerging teams.

What unites us is our willingness to create a better world for us and to pass it on to the coming generation. "Moral Re-Armament is the good road of an ideology inspired by God upon which all can unite. Catholic, Jew and Protestant, Hindu, Muslim, Buddhist and Confucianist- all find they can change, where needed, and travel along this good road together." - Frank Buchman.

What also unites us is the reflection time, which I define as a filter to support us in a continuous purification process. It can be defined in a different way from each one of us. But what is sure is that it is not an easy process, challenging all the temptations, but our fellowship is what makes us keep on going. When maintenance of our filter is needed there will be a highlight, support, friend to share with and then the repair may occur if it is our intention and will. Greed is what creates all those divisions, conflicts, dissatisfactions, so let's reflect together on Frank Buchman saying "There is enough in the world for everyone's need, but not enough for everyone's greed." What do you think about that?

IofC is not a movement, it is not perfection, no one is perfect and I do believe that we are all aware of that. As at several circumstances we do recognize that we are sinners, we have difficult characters, we may be at some point demanding, ungrateful, we may lose faith and hope and here again, our fellowship is a great reminder and support. "With them, I gladly shared my all and learned the great truth that where God guides, He provides." - F. Buchman.

What is preventing you from listening to the voice deep within you? What is this voice trying to tell you? What can you do to be able to listen to it? How to keep on challenging your personal transitions and mutation? How to be fully aware of all what is happening deep within?

CHAPTER FOURTEEN

More Transitions to Come

Writing this book has been a transition in itself, a new experience, will it lead to another transition again or will it stop here? While writing "The Power of Transitions" I voyaged through several ups and downs. I was hoping that by the end of this writing journey, I will embrace more certainty and clarity but I think, I have more horizons to be discovered. I need to be more flexible and keep faith at the highest level; the zenith. It is like life is communicating to me, "Get ready, and always expect new surprises. There may be new successes or new challenges or failures but I know that in all the cases, you will receive them openly". After accomplishing the coaching program what will happen? What about the master program, will I start it? Will it be the next chapter of the new transition? Will I find an internship? Will I go back to Lebanon and check for new job opportunities? Will I find a new contribution that I can offer? Or will I just start as a freelancer? How will be my inner transition keep on moving? How to create learnings from each transition? How to keep on walking into a continuous healing process? How to create daily satisfactions even during challenging time? What will be my next chapter about, let's be patient and everything will fall into order at the right moment, all that I have to do is play my part. "If opportunity doesn't knock, build a door."-Milton Berle.

While I write this book, we are still dealing with Aunty Coco (COVID-19), in some countries, the numbers are at an alarming rise. According to prevision, the second round may be harder than the previous one! The economic situation is in deficit and challenged worldwide but more in Lebanon. News shared are not really reassuring. There is a probability of living a new regional conflict that may become an international war. What will be the next transition, to write new destructions more than what we have already witnessed? What about our world, isn't it already suffocating? Was not Corona a sign of distress? How long will our world support all that we are doing? Any realization during COVID-19? What role can you play in creating a better world? How can you start? How to keep on moving toward your better self? How to radiate the divine power from deep within to the outer world? How to find out your higher purpose and walk toward it? How is that purpose serving the world? How ready are you for what will be to discover next in your journey?

"Start by doing what is necessary, then what is possible, and suddenly you are doing the impossible" - Francis of Assisi.

Lebanon is a big part of my roots, Gabon roots have been created with a lot of memories. Switzerland made me feel connected to a new lifestyle, it made me feel connected to a huge part of the world. Egypt with a big powerful fellowship, India colorful multicultural and in harmony; their service has a great meaning, Syria in the heart praying for more peace , Palestine a hope that will never die, Córdoba and the convivencia. I had the opportunity to visit different countries and feel a powerful connection with many.

Through the international programs physical when it was still possible before covid 19 and virtual now to adapt to the pandemic situation I do feel more connected. Each new experience taught me that wherever we are, we are connected. We are all passing through peaks and valleys. Every One is being challenged, some challenges are similar and others completely different. Our labelling and packaging may look different but within, we are all the same. In each one of us there is a Divine Power, an enlightened spirit. In each one of us, there is the same bubble of emotions. Will we decide to live with the spiritual light? Or navigate to selfishness; the tunnel of darkness? Are we ready and willing to start with personal changes? What can each one of us start with? How to create that change? What support do you need?

"Life is too short to wake up with regrets. So love the people who treat you right. Forget about those who don't. Believe everything happens for a reason. If you get a chance, take it. If it changes your life, let it. Nobody said life would be easy, they just promised it would most likely be worth it" - Harvey Mackay.

"Indeed, Allah will not change
the condition of a people until
they change what is in themselves."

*—**Al Raad,** 13:11, the Holy Quran*

Transitions

It is a mysterious journey
Surface is clear and wavy
Sunshine reflections daily
Drawn smile so let it be happy

Reflections of all what is external
Reflections of our society
Reflections but what is the reality?
Are outer reflections the same as
what is within you and me?

Lac, river, ocean or sea
What a great analogy
They appear to be always full of energy and vitality
But what is down deeply?

A big mystery!
Diving a skill for so many discoveries
Deeper we go peacefully
More it will be the creation of its harmony

A need to heal wounds of history
Celebrate achievements frequently
Learn always with flexibility
It will not be always easy

It is all about our life's journey
Meaning is in profundity
Daily we need to learn and dive deeply
Let's dive deeply, to find the purpose of our journey.

To know more about IofC,
you may click on the links below:

https://www.iofc.ch/

https://in.iofc.org/

https://www.iofc.org/

https://www.iofc.org/files/dynamics-change

https://www.facebook.com/iofcleb

Printed in Poland
by Amazon Fulfillment
Poland Sp. z o.o., Wrocław

26149087R00095